DORIS   *The Story of a Disfigured Deaf Child*

The Story of a Disfigured Deaf Child

by *Aron Ronald Bodenheimer, M.D.*
University of Tel Aviv Medical School

translated by Harold A. Basilius

Wayne State University Press   Detroit   1974

Supplement 2 to Acta Paedopsychiatrica, *Volume 35*
© *1968 by Schwabe and Co., Basel, Switzerland*

English translation © *1974 by Wayne State University Press,*
Detroit, Michigan 48202
Translated from the German by Harold A. Basilius.
Published simultaneously in Canada by The Copp Clark Publishing Co.,
517 Wellington Street, West, Toronto 2 B, Canada

Library of Congress Cataloging in Publication Data

Bodenheimer, Aron Ronald.
    Doris: the story of a disfigured deaf child.

    Translation of Doris: die Entwicklung einer
Beziehungsstörung und die Geschicht ihrer Behebung
bei einer entstellten, taubstummen Mädchen.
    Bibliography: p. 125
    1. Schizophrenia in children—Cases, clinical
reports, statistics. 2. Physically handicapped
children—Case studies. 3. Children, Deaf—Case
studies. 4. Child psychotherapy—Cases, clinical
reports, statistics. I. Title. [DNLM: 1. Abnor-
malities—Case studies. 2. Deafness—In infancy and
childhood.—Case studies. 3. Psychoses—In infancy and
childhood—Case studies. WM200 B663s 1973]
RJ506.S3   618.9′28′9043   72–11341
ISBN 0–8143–1495–3

Contents

Contents

16 illustrations are distributed throughout the text.

Preface

The following presentation resulted from a report given to the 143rd meeting of the Swiss Society for Psychiatry. The general theme of that meeting was "The Psychopathology of Expression," and following that theme, I presented the essential drawings made by Doris with my interpretations of them. That presentation enabled me to point out the uniqueness of Doris's illness and the special treatment developed for it. In discussions with colleagues following the presentation I was enabled to amplify many problems further and to discuss attempts at their solution more thoroughly.

This book is the result of those discussions, but, even more, of long collaboration with the officials in charge of the education and care of the deaf in Zurich. The particular case described here is representative of many—almost countless—other ailments and problems we have sought cooperatively to overcome, at times unsuccessfully but often successfully. Accordingly, I present this report as a token of my esteem for my colleagues.

I owe special thanks to Professor J. Lutz for including my manuscript in the *Series Paedopsychiatrica*.

DORIS   *The Story of a Disfigured Deaf Child*

I. Background

Somatic preconditions and family background

Doris, the little girl who is the subject of this report, is now (1968) thirteen years of age. Her appearance is striking. We can provide a precise description of her stigmatization; indeed we can give it a definite scientific name. The congenital affliction present in Doris as one sees her and as one hears her has been described by the pioneer investigators D. Klein[17] and P. J. Waardenburg.[24] The affliction is summarized as a syndrome bearing the names of these two scientists.

In his basic monograph Klein has summarized the distinguishing and specific characteristics of this dysmorphosis composed of ectodermal and mesodermal elements under the following six headings:

1. Localized albinism accompanied by blue eyes and a deaf-mute condition

2. Dyscrania (lack of the nasofrontal corner, broadened root of the nose, high gums, irregular tooth locations, and hypoplasia of the rami ascendentes of the lower jaw with retrognathia)

3. Antimongoloid diagonal slant of the eyelids; broadened distance of the inner and outer corners of the eyes with blepharophimosis (ancyloblepharon) and dystopia of the lower lacrimal points

4. Amyoplasia and gelenkstarre congenita of the upper extremities

5. Dysplasia of the entire bone system (the researcher deals extensively with the individual skeletal derangements)

6. Wing membrane in the area of the armpits and syndactylism.

The basic symptoms of the foregoing anomaly are present in Doris: First, her deafness; then the malformation of the skull designated as dyscrania; in terms of Klein's description we find in Doris the lack of the nasofrontal corner together with (considerable) broadening of the nasal root and a palatum ogivale with irregular bite formation. Retrognathia is not present. However, the child exhibits the localized albinism of the syndrome in the form of a continuous white streak running from about the base of the forehead through her black hair. The blue eyes noted by Klein would in and of themselves not constitute a symptom except that Doris has only one blue eye, the other being of a brownish color. Aside from the fact that this heterochromia, in addition to all the other misfortunes, also forebodes the later occurrence of a cataract—thus a visual impairment in addition to deafness—this heterochromous stigma exaggerates the shock occasioned by the girl's appearance. Above and beyond this, the antimongoloid slant of the eyelids is very apparent, just as one can observe the broadening of the distance between the outer and inner corners of the eyes combined with ancyloblepharon and a dystopia of the lower lacrimal points. Additionally, Doris manifests still another facial peculiarity (not mentioned by Klein), synophrys, that is, the growing together of the eyebrows, which by being joined together above the root of the nose constitute a prominent growth of black hair extending from the glabella to the middle of the nose bridge, thus accenting and caricaturing the deformed, flattened, and distorted nose, so prominently placed, as a physiognomic center.

It would doubtless have been easier to substitute some good photographs to illustrate my account. But for reasons I shall discuss later I decided against taking any pictures of the child. For the same reasons I did not investigate if or to what extent skeletal changes (in the sense of Klein's developmental disturbances) or cutical malformations were present in Doris.* I did learn from the head nurse that Doris's shoulders differed from those of other children, but neither the motility nor motoricity of her shoulder joints or other parts of her body was noticeably changed.

We were of the opinion that we could well afford to dispense with any thorough exploration of the morphological peculiarities of the girl inasmuch as any further data would not have contributed to the therapy.

If we now add to our information regarding the disturbances, that is, deafness and deformity, the fact that Doris was born out of wedlock and that her family situation from the start was such that a home was denied her, although her mother has now married, we might well recall the bitter words of Eugen Bleuler: "Let anyone who wants to be happy on this earth and eventually to get into heaven select the proper parents, because subsequently he cannot materially change the situation." [3a]

Kindergarten and early school years

Contrary to what one might assume from my description, Doris was neither especially striking nor notably difficult during the first years of her stay at the boarding school for the deaf (which she entered at the age of four). Even her physiognomic stigmatization appeared during kindergarten and early grade school years as an appealing and droll kind

* Klein later (1969) examined Doris at his own request and confirmed the diagnosis.

of oddity rather than as a repulsive disfigurement. And the conduct of the little girl corresponded to her appearance. Reports about her even include the word "sunshine." One of the nurses in her diary states: "When I look at her, I have to compare Doris to a little gypsy. She is nimble as a weasel and in addition quite roguish, often wild and high-spirited, and then in turn as clinging as a kitten."

The first noticeable disturbances in behavior were pronounced undesignated exertions which impressed her companions as ludicrous rather than sinister. The teacher at that time noted of the eight-year-old that "Dear old St. Nick is the sheerest bogeyman for Doris. She fears him very much though I constantly try to convince her that he obviously brings many fine gifts." The ominous threat then took full possession of the girl. "When St. Nick . . . appeared, the little girl tried again and again during the meal to control her arm lest she should actually raise it." Thus did fear penetrate the child through and through, through her bones, through her entire body. And yet one scarcely noticed it.

Even more serious than her profound fear, as reflected in her bodily sensations, are the bases of those sensations as they appear in the tree drawings, spontaneously executed, of the eight-year-old child: in the trunk rising from nowhere and leaving no room in the drawing for the ground or the roots; in the smoothly trimmed off branches having dried-up sprouts of foliage and completely lacking a crown; in the surface of the trunk which is not just shaded, not just spotted, but is represented as being completely compressed, almost in the manner of a relief.[8]

Despite these isolated manifestations that could later be easily interpreted as serious prodromes of a severe disturbance, the inclusion of the girl in her class and also in the group was so unobtrusive as to make unnecessary any special attention to these forewarnings, particularly since the teachers and supervisors at the Zurich school for the deaf know well how to cope with the behavioral disturbances that occur not infrequently among their students.

The change-over

First phase: insolence, shamelessness

The sudden radical change followed by only a few weeks the onset of menstruation. Indeed, the child's appearance changed very quickly: her droll yet peculiarly charming doll-like face, despite its distortion, coarsened; her movements became disordered and seemed at times almost ataxic.

Tragically but significantly the severe disturbances first centered about the disfigurement which was rapidly becoming accentuated: when the girl returned from home to school on Monday mornings by train, she knew precisely where to place herself in the coach so as to interfere most effectively with the circulation of the other passengers. She took up her position at this very point in a manner fixed and motionless, thus compelling her fellow passengers to squeeze past. At such moments her face assumed a downright mischievous and malicious look, according to the consensus of the other passengers. The same kind of thing occurred frequently at various places and in other situations. When Doris left the deaf-mute school to attend gym class in a municipal school, she managed to annoy the children enjoying their recess in the schoolyard to such an extent that they beat her up several times (this despite the fact that these children were generally well behaved in the presence of their deaf schoolmates, even friendly to them).

The impression is truly inescapable that Doris was anticipating in the people she casually encountered the attitude which she obviously expected from them as a reaction to her appearance—indeed, no other kind of attitude could really "be anticipated." But it also seemed that though the girl on her part was rejecting, she in so doing was also defending herself against rejection—indeed, she was adopting the only available means for preventing rejection.

We encounter this mode of conduct in the essential context of the accelerated disfigurement of the face with great and, in my judgment, regular frequency: that kind of conduct which functions as a provocation and strikes one as a provocation without any anticipation of consequences is, in short, insolence. *Insolence* rather than spitefulness is the proper term for this kind of conduct because it is unquestionably directed against not *reacting*—indeed, never letting the situation reach the point of reaction—but rather *acting*, that is, keeping the initiative to act.

A second frame of reference makes it necessary for us to regard Doris's behavior as a manifestation of insolence, namely, her exhibitionism, and that means her deliberately intruding and protruding that face of hers which I on my part had never looked for. This is the behavior we commonly call insolence.

From those two observations a third one results that enables us to understand the essence of insolence and the particular kind of insolence we are concerned with here: anyone who acts superior, that is, anyone who by means of his face provokes the gaze of another but lacks concurrence in that superiority by the person he is confronting, is insolent. But we may also regard this kind of conduct as shamelessness in its purest and most elementary form.

The case of our little patient lends a special coloration to her shamelessness by transferring it to her distorted face. The transfer enables us to some extent to understand the particular tragedy and problems of her case. We shall have occasion to return to this matter.

It may be superfluous in this connection to pursue the question of whether we are dealing with a conscious or an unconscious act. The situation with which we are "literally" confronted here is removed from the framework of reference based upon the ordinary concepts of "consciousness" or of "being conscious" and "unconsciousness."

Second phase: withdrawal

Impudent conduct of the kind mentioned can develop over a longer period of time during and after acute facial distortion (as I have sought to show in another context),[9] then ultimately consolidate, and indeed become habitual. In Doris's case the impudence maintained itself for only a short period, scarcely a month (though it continued to reappear temporarily again and again and in unique ways). Actually, it was a kind of middle phase in her development. The reaction to this kind of conduct on the part of the child was so intense—perhaps we ought now to say "fortunately"—that the transition from provocative, insolent conduct to the next phase, namely, withdrawal, occurred quickly—not simple resignation, to be sure, but withdrawal interspersed with recurring acts of protestation.

The supervisor provides an excellent description of Doris's conduct in telegraphic style during this latter 'phase: "Extremely off balance . . . cries and howls or acts defiant like a small child . . . suddenly disappears on one occasion from the living room and hides herself away in bed like a small animal . . . seldom lies in bed in normal fashion, however, so that one can scarcely see her. Tosses herself about . . . frequently back and forth. She refuses to greet me in the morning or even to get up and is morose and sullen. This flight into bed and 'leave me alone' phase lasted a couple of months."

This sullen, withdrawn attitude is accompanied by another which seems diametrically opposite: "Suddenly commences, particularly toward evening, to become restless, loud and high-spirited. She refuses to go to bed and complains that she can't sleep. I try to dissuade her . . . I sometimes take her to my room for a little while and then put her to bed. However, she refuses to go to bed but instead lies down on the floor back of the door and almost falls asleep."

"I admit that I found the girl repugnant at this time and that I had to force myself to accept her just as she was." This casual but significant observation in the report of the supervisor seems to occur only casually in context with that extraordinary and contradictory conduct of the child—her inclination to withdraw, on the one hand, and her desire to relate and even to impose herself on her supervisor, on the other.

The girl's suffering became more acute from day to day, and with it so did the concern and the feeling of helplessness on the part of the supervisor. The latter noted: "The evenings are becoming more and more critical whereas the situation remains a little more normal during the day. Complains more frequently about stomachache and lacks appetite. Commences . . . to cry out in long drawn out huuh-sounds. Repeatedly turns on the lights in the bedroom when the other children want to sleep. Mentions for the first time that she is afraid of her dreams: 'The devil comes and eats flesh and blood. I have often dreamed of the devil coming. I'm scared.'

"I can calm her down, but as soon as she is back in bed, she starts to howl and whimper and toss about. Scarcely lies still a minute, trembles all over or tosses about continuously. Breaks out in cold sweat. Tells me her heart is palpitating, her hands and feet are ice-cold. . . .

"Next night she refuses to go to bed, hides in the staircase hall. Is defiant but also despondent and terrified. Says she is no longer afraid of the devil but she might dream about some catastrophe, a train might derail or a bridge collapse . . . she dreams this way again and again. She doesn't calm down till eleven o'clock. I sit beside her in the room and try continuously to leave her alone . . . she is simply in the grip of her fear. On one occasion I hear her saying her goodnight prayer aloud several times.

"The disturbance increases from day to day. Every evening she repeats: 'I'm afraid, I'm scared, I don't want to go to bed.' Lies down in the hallway, tosses herself about, or pushes herself around lying on the floor. After about a week I bed her down on a mattress in the living room and give her a night-stand lamp. The doors are always kept open till she falls asleep. But when finally I turn the light out, she cries out again and wants to detain me."

A few days later the report notes: "she's spiteful and malicious; when I want to talk to her, she hides her face and refuses to listen to me (that is, to read my lips and continue to communicate with me). Is aware, however, that I stand helpless before her if she refuses to look at my mouth." And the supervisor interprets the child's behavior: "Obviously not to be reached by means of language, obdurate, 'deaf.' " * And immediately thereupon and again seemingly unrelated to the foregoing: "I force her (inasmuch as she refuses to let anyone see her undressed) to remove her clothing and go to bed."

The girl tries over and over again to find her way to the other children, but she always fails to do so. "Thus her fears grow," the report continues, "when five other girls are in the room with her."

Doris's psychosis as a relational disturbance

This concise statement primarily in terms of Doris's supervisor's reports reveals the development of a psychotic condition and then the sudden shift into actual psychotic alienation. Like so much else in human behavior, the deaf

* In Swiss-German, *deaf* [*taub*] means both "unable to hear" and "bad," "creating ill-will," or even "mad."

person in the process of developing a psychosis demonstrates in a particularly incisive and paradigmatic way what goes on inside human beings and among human beings in their interrelationships to one another and in the disturbance of these relationships:

The child is compelled to seek himself among others in order to find himself, to identify himself. When rejected, he rejects in turn, thus avoiding further rejections: he becomes insolent. However, he is unable to tolerate his own insolence, his isolation, and the forlornness into which he has fallen, and thus he reveals the great, consuming anxiety to which he has become victim just as any human being does when he fails to get any answer or the wrong answer to his appeal from another person. This phase of anxiety is experienced, recognized, and reacted to through talking, whimpering, dreaming of the devil and blood, and through countless conversional phenomena such as sweating, palpitations, loss of appetite and retching, and by wailing and excessive dependence which, though they are frequently manifested as imposition, can yet be experienced and accepted by attendants as an "acceptable" symptom of need.

It is obvious, however, that Doris "felt" that she, as she was—that is, as those around her experienced her and as they took an attitude toward her—could not gain acceptance or at best could do so only by means of great self-control, despite the enormous patience and devotion she got from her supervisor Miss Hüberli. It became increasingly more evident that Doris eschewed patience and devotion. She sought to be accepted and to be able to stand on her own. Above all she desired the privilege of herself deciding if and whom she wanted to accept or reject. In other words, she sought an opportunity to come to terms with herself. Since this opportunity was not open to her, the behavior of the child changed once again. In this, her third phase, Doris became "spiteful and malicious," in the words of her teacher.

(Actually, as we shall learn later, it would be more accurate to speak of *rancor* rather than *spitefulness*.)

This shift in the girl's behavior immediately brought about a corresponding change of attitude on the part of persons surrounding her. That a human being is suffering is readily conceded, however, only so long as the manner in which the suffering is manifested remains in conformity with the notions we have of suffering. All that transpired in the second phase—no matter how much sympathy and patience it occasioned—conformed to generally accepted notions. It could therefore be regarded as suffering. The sufferer was allowed to cry out, to entertain anxiety, to express it, and to discuss it; she could even be obtrusive. All of this corresponds to the well-known image of suffering.

Only the frankness of the teacher enabled her to express clearly and uncompromisingly the change to what was no longer permissible by means of the two unambiguous words *spiteful* and, more significantly, *malicious*. Either a person is suffering—one may hypostatize this condition also thus: either a person is sick—or he is spiteful and malicious. These are the alternatives and they do not lend themselves to compromise.

We have learned meantime when the transition from suffering to maliciousness occurred. The shift is expressed in the statement already quoted: "Is spiteful and malicious; when I want to talk to her, she covers up her face and refuses to listen to me. . . ." Spitefulness, that is, rancor, and maliciousness could scarcely be manifested in so basic and recognizable a manner, thus revealing in such direct and elementary fashion their very essence, as in the situation of this deaf and disfigured girl. The statement, cited earlier, proves all this. But even better, the sentence following: "She knows that I (the supervisor) am helpless in her presence."

To return to the shift: until this very moment Doris was the helpless child in need of protection. Now, however, by her conduct, she caused her teacher to become helpless, confused, and ashamed; indeed she made her teacher, who had formerly remained independent in her helplessness regardless of the cost, dependent upon her, Doris. By means of this observation the teacher with remarkable astuteness involuntarily designated one of the basic circumstances under which the gradual shift into psychosis occurs.

Doris in various ways exemplifies and accentuates the situation whereby the nurse becomes a dependent: Doris clings so tightly to her teacher that the latter becomes concerned about her own absolute independence and correspondingly feels uncomfortable. Simultaneously, however, and by this very means, the child withdraws from genuine relationship. Her desperately clinging manner makes it impossible for Doris and her nurse to have feeling for each other. That kind of desperate clinging destroys every kind of reciprocal feeling. And even if the nurse still attempts to resume a relationship with the girl, it is destroyed from the start because the girl rejects her in no uncertain terms: Doris covers up her face, becomes stubborn, refuses to "hear" (hearing is, of course, identical with seeing in the case of the deaf girl), and refuses to let herself be heard. She does not even let herself be seen anymore. Evenings she crawls off somewhere when she is supposed to go to bed. She refuses to undress because she does not want her nurse to see her in that state. Not hearing or being heard, not seeing or being seen, the child now withdraws completely.

At this time, the nurse, experienced in dealing with the deaf, had occasion by means of a single word to allude to the ancient, all-inclusive insight attached to the small word "deaf" [*taub*], namely, the relation of the incapacity for hearing to being furious, indeed, even to being mad. This ancient semantic association of two disparate situations which seem to have nothing in common in any practical sense (an association energetically and vehemently rejected by all who are interested in deaf people) is wiser than everyday language about the implications of "deafness" as a totality: the inability to hear [*nicht-hören*] another person, the inability to perceive what someone standing before you is saying, does not by itself constitute the essence of deafness, which, strictly interpreted, does not make the inability to hear identical with deafness. Only the absence of the ability (that is, the lack of the readiness) to be heard by another person and—which is the same thing—by means of the other's reply to hear one's self constitute deafness in the comprehensive sense implied by language. But there is still another aspect which necessarily results from this change of relationship. If hearing and hearing one's self [*sich-anhören*] are nonexistent, that is to say, if the relationship ceases [*auf-hören*], a new situation necessarily develops, namely, the situation of listening to one's self [*sich-zuhören*]. The person listening to himself is now completely dependent upon himself and listens only to whatever goes on within himself. This kind of tendency can develop in any human being, not only in deaf persons, though the latter are obviously in greater danger of thus gliding into a state of listening to themselves and excluding all others. Listening to one's self, which is perhaps best understood as a kind of listening from within, is always latent and only waits for the opportunity to become dominant as a result of the disappearance of one's hearing one's self.[12]

In this respect the hearing person and the deaf one behave similarly, and this circumstance is also the only one through which hearing persons can gain an understanding of how a deaf person lives and experiences life. Otherwise we only understand how a deaf person is different from us, and the question really is, how can we come into a relationship with a person who really is in the same life situation as our own.

The first indication of what, still unorganized, happens in

listening to one's self occurs from the noise we hear resulting from our yawning.

Thus, *auf-hören* has two meanings, that is, *turning the ear,* which seems to indicate the fact of hearing by means of showing the hearing organ; actually, however, the meaning is *averting* or *warding off,* which is indicated by averting one's face and thereby converting the *hearing OF one's self* (*sich-ANhören* which is implicitly outer directed) into the *listening TO one's self* (*sich-ZUhören*). The latter act may well remain unstructured though it tends to want to structure itself just as everything unstructured in life does. Whereupon that which is perceived in a dull and sensuous fashion is converted into language. In psychiatric terms, the acousmas or auditory hallucinations are transformed into auditive, that is, linguistic hallucinations.[12]

In trying to prevent the tendency I have described, the teacher and psychotherapist have the same intent. The only difference is in procedure.

The course of Doris's self-isolation was a tragic experience, and the developments as recorded by her teacher were very impressive: first, the provocation of reactions from without, then the screaming and whining, and thereupon, though less differentiated, the inarticulate uuh-sounds, all calculated to attract attention, to hear herself, and finally then the aversion, the "spite," the withdrawal (*Täubi,* as Swiss-German expresses it so effectively).

The little girl reveals this development with special intensity because her disfigurement does not allow her to experience visually what she has experienced auditively. At the start of the psychosis the girl imposes her deformed face upon the people about her. She compels them to look at her and thereby preempts their role of being looked at and looked over. She does this in a provocative manner, but it is precisely by this kind of challenge that she attains her goal, by means of her own "looking back." By her own glance she forbids the looking of the others, and the more malicious and spiteful her glances can be made to challenge the eyes of her "opponents," the more effective and dominant is her banishment of their looking. They are simply not prepared to encounter her malicious glances. The girl subdues her "opponents," and they hold that fact against her.

That, however, is only the initial phase. Now Doris abdicates. The fact of her resignation is manifested by her withdrawal. She averts her face from everyone and covers her disfigured countenance with both hands.

In this process the fact is not only the locus of seeing but simultaneously and essentially the means also of being seen. Averting the face prevents not only seeing but being seen as well. This is the reason, of course, why man puts on clothes, namely, to concentrate the looks of those about him on his *face*.[12] A naked person can accomplish the same end, provided of course his glance is sufficiently strong to meet and hold that of the other fellow, which may be wandering over the entire body. The situation of the disfigured and resigned child is quite different. She is no longer able to repulse the glances of the others. The locus to be viewed and the locus from which viewing originates are obviously sick, much more so than if the girl were blind.[10] She is helpless even when clothed, but if she were naked, she would be completely defenseless and helplessly exposed to "the evil rays" of the strange glances. Such a person, such a child, if unclothed, is utterly and profoundly naked. That is why Doris cannot undress herself in the evening when she is supposed to go to bed.

This conception of facial disfigurement aids us in comprehending why we should not attempt to understand the essence of deformity in the universal sense of one of the many available "psychologies of handicapped persons" or "psychologies of the sensorially deprived." Above all, however, we shall never comprehend the tragedy and the problems with which Doris overwhelms us, if we attribute the particular nature of her ills to an organic deficiency which may be (inadequately) compensated for.[1]

Distortion of the face at the locus of seeing and being seen, that *is* Doris. Accordingly, her situation is not comparable to the case of a fourteen-year-old patient called Max described by Hans Zulliger with singular capacity as an example for combining goodness with determination.[25] Max lost a leg as the result of an accident. He quickly learned how to adjust to his defect; indeed, he played it for all it was worth. Even more, he became a thief and proceeded to store his loot in the empty pants leg covering his stump. Who would have the idea—who would have had the fortitude—of looking for stolen goods in such a "taboo" location?

Young Max's and Doris's problems are quite different. A child can "divorce" himself from a damaged leg, if he *has* one. And Max with his stub can accordingly manage in very different fashion from Doris, who *is* her disfigured face. A commonplace, though no less important and often overlooked, fact indicates that a human being cannot be what he has, and conversely he cannot do what he wishes with what he is, because he does not have it.[12] Therein lies the tragedy of little Doris.

The unsuccessful therapy of Zulliger in the case of young Max (about which Zulliger, one of the founders of and a professional in child psychotherapy, reports so impressively) may perhaps be traced to Zulliger's failure to pay sufficient attention to the ugly specific problems of the disturbed relationship imposed upon us by a boy who has suffered the loss of a leg even though that disturbance be different from that of a deaf girl with a disfigured face.

The stage of the stormy psychosis

Doris's agitation now becomes more and more exaggerated and disturbing. Her every other word is "fear, fear." In the evening she lies down on the floor, wherever she may be, not in her bed. Her frozen and empty stare is apparent to everyone, and her attendants confess that they are afraid of her and that their fear of her greatly exceeds their anxiety about her. The chief reason for their concern is her unpredictability. When Doris wants to seesaw and the seesaw is not available, she behaves "like a very little girl," and it is impossible to dissuade her from her wish; her stiff posture dissolves into strange and extraordinary laughter. During recess Doris "intentionally" throws a ball at the head of her attendant, and reverts to her strange, frightening look.

At night when Doris finally falls asleep, she is tormented by dreams. Her "normal" dreams project people being laughed at because they are ugly. Her "bad" dreams involve her taking a walk when suddenly a loud bang occurs and everybody falls down dead.

For a long time, the child had not been permitted to go to her home for the weekend. Doris herself asked for permission to stay at school. Previously, when Doris became disturbed and afraid, her mother and half-sisters would often gather about her and be greatly amused by her behavior.

Her best moments are in class, though her class performance is no longer on the same level as that of the earlier industrious student. But discipline still provides Doris with some stability, and when she does become loud, her teacher speaks even louder. Sometimes the explosion takes place during recess.

The diagnosis that Doris was sick did not originate with her doctor or with her teachers and attendants. Instead, it was her fellow students in this school for deaf-mutes who perceived the profound changes the girl had undergone. At first they attempted to stand by Doris but were "disappointed when they failed" (Hüberli). Additional observations of the group leader: "One of the girls compares Doris to F. K." (a deeply disturbed boy in the kindergarten of the school who attacked the other children and constantly destroyed their busywork). Another remarked: "Too bad that Doris has suddenly become very ill."

II. Therapy

Therapeutic possibilities: basic considerations

At this point, I was consulted about the following considerations: the enormous restlessness of the child which threatened to affect the other inmates of the school, especially the resident ones; her increasing rejection of nourishment, carefully recorded with great concern by the supervisor; the imminent transformation of participation into aversion and (what is worse) anxiety on the part of the other children; comparable disturbances among the teaching and nursing personnel; the fear on the part of the administration of an event, no telling what, extremely dangerous to Doris herself and perhaps also to the other children—all of these matters demanded immediate and effective action.

It was apparent that the question of whether Doris could be permitted to remain in our school and be treated there had fateful implications. Removing Doris from these familiar surroundings and from contact with other deaf persons to a psychiatric institute, in a location strange to her, no matter how carefully the transfer might be effected, could possibly lead to a complete and definitive psychotic regression.

Since the administration of the school consulted me about Doris, I became acquainted with the problems of her case simply because I had become associated with people entrusted with the child's care, even before I had done anything at all or given any kind of counsel. Once I became involved in the case, I had to regard myself as a responsible party together with those of the school.

No psychiatric-psychotherapeutic counsellor can in my view dissociate himself from that kind of function. It provides not only relief for all parties concerned but also an assurance and freedom regarding one's own conduct. We are concerned here not only because "someone should be present in case something happens," important and justified as that requirement is for the presence of the physician, but also because this kind of concern contributes to the maintenance of a high level of responsibility among the other personnel.

Note, however, that involvement and responsibility can bring with them very real and very sensitive demands that at times can threaten the reputation of the therapist as, for example, when following some actual incident, criticisms are voiced by the parents of other deaf children, by foreign visitors, by organizations, or by journalists. The therapist who decides to exchange his safe position behind the couch temporarily for other locations and thereby substitute unquestionable "dirty work" for his "clean work" (W. Hoffer)* obviously runs this risk.

Two leading factors

The psychotherapy involved here was determined from the very beginning by two factors, namely, the structure of Doris's school, that is, the attitude of the teachers, the supervisor, and her fellow students toward the child, and the peculiar nature of Doris's affliction.

* A remark made in a discussion group of the Swiss Medical Society for Psychotherapy, Zurich, 1960.

Presuppositions about the school

The individual authorities of the school
and the attitude of the school toward the children

We can state that the structure of the school in its present form is representative of a liberal institution inasmuch as conversations among the various responsible persons, especially the administration, the teachers, and the supervisors, are frequently and, indeed, usually possible. Emotional difficulties, disagreements regarding questions of competence, competition for the favor of the children or their parents, all these phenomena are observable without exception in all resident schools and are therefore also present in our deaf-mute school in Zurich. The point, however, is not that such disturbances are nipped in the bud. That would be possible only in a completely sterile, disinterested educational community. Instead, the health of the teaching group working therapeutically is demonstrated insofar as the tendency toward open reciprocal discussions and public communication between the individual personnel holds to a minimum any injurious effect on the children, and also insofar as such discussions involve the expressions of individuals and not the demands of rigidly constituted special interest groups such as the teachers or supervisors. Not the least of the tasks incumbent upon the psychotherapeutic consultant of such an organization in my view are the preservation and nurturing of such spontaneous discussions.[21]

It would hardly have been possible for us to handle Doris within the framework of our school, if the above situation had not existed. Without such a school situation, the first precondition for dealing with Doris would have been doubtful, namely, the possibility of making available to her a pleasure in motherly care and patience and love in addition to the firm stance of a demanding but tolerant and restrained teacher. Both of these were equally significant for this deeply frightened child, devoid of all inward as well as outward controls. It is not at all self-evident that the two available advantages, both representing parental principle, could cooperate without conflicting with each other. It was our good fortune to have two unusually perceptive people, a supervisor Miss U. Hüberli and a teacher Mr. E. Pachlatko, who were constantly amenable to Doris, to each other, and to the suggestions of the physician. I was from the first more concerned with the recommendations of these two attendants of Doris, with my discussions with them, and with encouraging their activities than with my own endeavors.[15,21]

The relation of the psychotherapist to these authorities

The longer I serve as a therapeutic counsellor, the more appropriate does the attitude mentioned above seem to me for the function of an educational institution. Also it seems more important to me than does the intervention of the counsellor in the interest of individual children. By this means and from the beginning, the divergence so commonly observable between teachers and therapist (who then so often regards himself sorrowfully as the victim of misunderstanding, of ignorance, of inadequate information, and of inhumanity) is eliminated. By this means we also avoid the otherwise common sabotage of the counsellor's suggestions and decisions. Above all, however, by this kind of procedure a much "more natural" kind of therapy becomes available to the child (because it is transmitted by way of the milieu to which the child is accustomed) by persons the child sees throughout the entire week, day and night, and not just for a few hours. Above and beyond all this a genuine therapeutic atmosphere develops that remains effective and helpful, far beyond the ever-present problematic individual case, for the other children of the institution, both the healthy and the afflicted ones. Thus the individual treatment becomes an exemplary situation rather than a showcase example.

Physician and "mother figure"

Intensive consultation with the various attendants of the girl and with their colleagues seemed mandatory if only because the head nurse suggested a treatment of Doris that required much more attention than was generally within the range of duties, indeed within the competence, of the teacher of a girl in complete pubertal development.

The situation was not made easier because from the very start, and not without intent, it was decided to dispense with any kind of symbolical explanation or other psychological interpretation of the role of Miss Hüberli, so that every effort to support the spontaneity of the teacher could be made more effective. Everything Miss Hüberli did should retain the character of directness and immediacy, and especially should not except tendencies on her part toward sympathy or antipathy or any discussions thereof in the presence of the physician. On the contrary, no irresponsible, impersonal reservations should be sought in the theory. Accordingly, it became clear that all of the colleagues among the teachers needed to be instructed about Doris's situation and related problems from the very beginning of the therapy, so as to anticipate adequately and neutralize the suspicions which the intensity of attention might foster. In view of certain incidents that had occurred at this time in a number of Swiss educational institutions, the danger of such misinterpretations of Miss Hüberli's conduct was unusually great.

The group to which Doris was assigned during recess periods included eleven other girls of various ages. It was necessary continuously to observe and compensate for the interactions occasioned by Doris's behavior and the (unintentional, yet easily observable) special attention she got from the supervisor. It happened that at that time I was concerned with a number of children in that same group, while on my part evading any public commitment to Doris.

Any such public commitment could have resulted in a greater isolation for Doris than all of her psychotic utterances and acts.

To be sure, it was very hard to devote attention to the resistance that Doris was creating for herself with such grimly tragic effect. In the continuing effort, therefore, to accept the contortions and distortions with which Doris—equally in her appearance and behavior—made things difficult for her environment, lay one of the greatest difficulties of the therapy.

In this connection I wish to emphasize an observation dealing with another basic and painful matter, namely, the obvious fact of the rarity of psychological conceptions, and the even greater rarity of articles about psychotherapeutic treatment which discuss, especially in visual terms, the appearance of the patient, that is, the way he looks. One might conclude that the appearance of a patient played no part in this therapy, but such a conclusion would be false. In neglecting the "appearance" factor and its significance for psychotherapy we are constrained to recognize the manifestation of a taboo. The patient's appearance proves extremely important not only to decide whether or not the therapy is successful, and this especially in the case of a female patient with a male therapist, but, much more important, to decide whether or not to initiate a therapy. This fact is generally evaded, overlooked, or buried in psychological considerations, and even phenomenology, the "theory of appearances," pursues paths other than the premise of relationship involved in every appearance. If we look more closely at reports about therapies of "pretty young girls," we frequently find comments that make us realize how much the selection, which is basic to the recommendation for therapy even though it may not be realized, revolved about the appearance of the patient. It is debatable whether or not this view results merely from the inclination to protect beauty from chronic illness.*

However that may be, ugliness confuses prognosis to a considerable degree in regard to psychotherapy, a regrettable fact that may lose some of its "compelling objectivity," once it has been realized and conceded.

The first and highly significant consequence of that concession leads to the revision of a prevailing psychiatric clinical mode of thought. We incline to correlate peculiarities of behavior, so common among disfigured persons, willy-nilly as partial phenomena ("symptomatic subgroups," so to speak), with the clinical syndromes (especially when the latter are connected with endocrine disturbances). This procedure is an easy one, particularly when it seems completely correct to the "critical observer," and one is unable to come up with logical and cogent arguments against it. If it is decided meanwhile to accept for therapy a disturbed child of the type described, one becomes involved in a highly illogical procedure and must accordingly be prepared to desist from correlating behavioral disturbances with the total syndrome. One of the first "sinful" aberrances, but not the only one, of a psychotherapy such as the one I am describing relates to the "destruction of the syndrome," at least insofar as its "psychic components" are concerned, that is, to the relinquishment of faith in the compelling relationships of the syndrome.

We have described Doris's appearance thoroughly. We need scarcely remark here that much preparation and patience on the part of the teacher are requisite to remain well disposed to that kind of child. All the more so because from the very beginning of her psychosis Doris emphasized

---

* Incidentally, psychotherapy is not the only discipline subscribing to this, I am tempted to say, "hedonistic" aestheticizing conception. The do-good societies are also suffused with it. Just take a look at the placards propagating support for the retarded. If on rare occasion they depict a disfigured face, that face must at least reflect "beautiful, expressive eyes." Basically, there has been no departure from the thesis of Lavater's Physiognomic Fragments according to which "a visible harmony exists between moral and corporeal beauty, and between moral and corporeal ugliness." (Cited according to Feuchtersleben.)[14]

her disfigurement by grimaces and physical distortions of the most ludicrous kind and gave it prominence in a very sinister way by the loud, animal-like huu-cries and other sounds of her hoarse voice, which was all the more noticeable in a community of children who were born deaf or became deaf at an early age.

Additionally at this time another development, an extremely painful one, occurred which made our relationship to the girl even more difficult. Her disturbances in the auditory and visual areas were further complicated by a pronounced body odor, probably occasioned by a secretion of the sebaceous glands, and this odor, characteristically, could not be materially reduced by hygienic means. Thus, the relational disturbance entered also into the osmatic area, that is, into a sphere that could disturb the relation in a most dangerous way, because in it the relationship if disturbed could withdraw most easily from discretion and realization, that is, from "consciousness."

To calculate the significance of relational disturbance in the osmatic area, we must remember the manner in which such a disturbance functions when it is removed from consciousness and not immediately accessible. We can do this only by a comparison with other kinds of disturbed relationships. It is possible to understand and to "empathize" the experience of blindness and to empathize the experience of hearing difficulty or deafness, though the latter is more difficult. Accordingly, it is possible by means of discretion and realization, i.e., "consciously," to come to grips with those relational disturbances. It is also possible to achieve this with a disfigured patient, and, subsequent to the initial irritation, an intelligent confrontation is possible. And even though the arousal of sympathy or antipathy is not readily available to discretion, it is at least available to realization. I can have only a limited influence on whether someone is sympathetic or unsympathetic toward me, but I can at the very least realize why someone is not sympathetic. However, the situation is quite different in an osmatically conditioned relational disturbance, because the latter is for the most part not amenable either to discretion or to realization. I cannot influence the arousal of sympathy or antipathy in this kind of situation, indeed, I ordinarily cannot realize either of them. I cannot even be certain whether an osmatic disturbance exists and is functioning between us, between me and the person confronting me.

The special tragedy and problem of this situation are accentuated further because the disturbance occurs reciprocally. Discretion and realization are denied both to the person perceiving the odor and the person emitting it. I cannot influence the way my body smells anymore than I can consciously realize whether or not I am emitting an odor and how this odor is perceived by others. Both the emitter and the perceiver of the odor are exposed to it.*

It was possible to discuss all these matters openly and freely with Miss Hüberli, and the discussions benefited greatly because, as is evidenced by the cited passages from her notes, she could admit her difficulties with Doris and did not need to embellish her aversion with affability.

Physician and "father figure"

The problem was, nevertheless, no easier for the girl's teacher. First, it involved keeping Doris in class despite the crude disruptions and difficulties occasioned by her conduct in class. No less important was the fact that Mr. Pachlatko remained consistent in attitude toward Doris, that is, he was not just content to operate with a comfortable and, so far as he was personally involved, irresponsible concept of illness, but instead accepted and tolerated the crude disturbances

---

* These facts are analyzed and discussed in a more detailed fashion in my *Versuch über die Elemente der Beziehung*,[12] but are mentioned here only briefly so that textual continuity is not destroyed.

which Doris imposed upon the class. Keeping in mind that at this time Doris simply "was not there" for hours during class, one can readily imagine the patience required by the teacher to carry on. I should like to emphasize that what the teacher did in this situation was to practice unadulterated pedagogy and nothing but pedagogy completely free of psychology and psychotherapy. Of course, Mr. Pachlatko was kept continuously and completely informed about Doris's problems but was never in any way "advised" to do this or to desist from doing that. The teacher was supposed to retain his impartiality and above all never to get the impression that his teaching was in the service of psychotherapy. The orderliness the girl enjoyed in her classes had the same priority as the psychotherapeutic aim to penetrate her peculiarities.

In the countless discussions with the teacher and the group leader, discussions undertaken for the most part with each of them separately, we again had opportunities to remind ourselves of the great importance for the psychotherapy of the deaf of the self-evident but often forgotten rule that non-deaf persons must never in the presence of the deaf discuss them or any other subject in such a way that these matters cannot be understood by them. Again and again forgetfulness, indifference, or that feeling of superiority that can insinuate itself so easily in the non-deaf do violence to the foregoing rule but not without great damage to the relationship to the deaf.

To the outsider this precept may seem to be an obvious truism and we have to grant that. But only those who spend much time with the deaf can appreciate how really difficult it is to remember the truism and to act accordingly, and how prone we are to violate this basic precept in dealing with the deaf.

On the contrary, very personal problems of deaf individuals may and can be dealt with in their presence, with or without their participation, even if only with the one proviso that the deaf person understands what is going on.

The special obligations of the psychotherapist

The psychiatric aspect of the problem and the diagnosis

My own obligation as therapist I found to be determined by the peculiarity of Doris's illness. A psychiatric diagnosis was not possible. Diagnostic clarification or "deepening" [*Vertiefung*] would also not provide any direction for the therapy. There was, therefore, no reason to suggest further diagnostic procedures regardless of their dimensions. Above all we had to avoid the temptation of regarding the psychosis as a partial manifestation of an ectodermal disturbance, that is, as a congenitally conditioned and therefore essentially untreatable malignancy.

Nonetheless, the nature of the "exceptional circumstances" required clarification. When Doris was found lying on the floor apparently disoriented and incapable of communicating but continuously shouting "why? why?", some kind of epileptic affliction was ultimately suggested. According to the teacher's description it seemed impossible with any certainty to undertake the diagnosis of that kind of affliction. Not until I had witnessed her in that kind of situation could I rule out the possibility of an illness related to epilepsy. Doris was incommunicable; she withdrew herself completely and actively from all efforts to investigate her "why? why?"; her movements had nothing convulsive about them; they merely indicated an intense rejection; and all the while she had complete recollection of everything that had happened at those times. Furthermore, any other manifestations which might indicate major or minor illness were not in evidence.

I shall no longer consider the consequences of a diagnosis indicating an epileptic affliction nor if such a diagnosis would have excluded psychotherapeutic treatment.

The "exceptional circumstance" which I witnessed only once—and then only its very end—had a frightening effect. One got the impression that Doris had already retreated deep into autism. After the start of the therapy the exceptional circumstances mentioned did not recur, but because of my provocation assumed their more natural forms. More about this later.

Since any additional diagnostic measures, which would have to indicate that no directly effective therapeutic consequence would result, would have been not helpful but damaging, we also decided against taking an electroencephalogram.[1]

The situation before us, that *was* the diagnosis; the diagnosis and the child who was diagnosed—the human being and her suffering—were one and the same: a disfigured, deaf child who, deeply afflicted in relational terms, now destroyed all remaining possibilities to relate. One unfortunately encounters this tendency not infrequently in extreme cases of elementary relational disturbances.* Indeed, the tendency is part of its condition, and special efforts and subtlety are required to retard its further development.

To isolate the specifics of this disturbance from other psychoses makes little sense and contributes little understanding, but, on the contrary, the analysis of the problems and the needs of this form of isolation help us to understand every psychosis, that is to say, psychosis in general.

What happened to Doris before the eyes of her teacher constituted a *thrust* [*Schub*] in the original and peculiar sense of that word. When we say *thrust*—fully aware that reservations are justified because misinterpretations are easily associated with the term—we exclude the question of "en-

* By "elementary relational disturbance" is meant every relational affliction which, even before any other communicational disturbances have occurred, is immediately present in the first encounter and which then becomes effective in whatever "first occurs" relationally, that is, in its elements, and which bursts out with immediacy and forcefulness, thus with an elementary intensity.

dogeny" or "reactivity." The question of "cause" is also eliminated by the concept *thrust,* if we interpret it straightforwardly. Nothing or nobody actually *thrusts* in the situation of the *thrust.* The essence of the thrust lies rather in a shift or displacement [*Verschiebung*]. Whenever the harmony of the development is disturbed in such a way that a discrepancy arises between its separate factors, we have a *thrust.*

Doris had precisely this kind of experience. Her dislocation developed now because with the advent of puberty the peculiar nature of the girl was first revealed clearly and forcefully. When Doris was still a little girl, her behavior had a comical and amusing effect and could thus be ignored in a playful way, but in the grown-up girl such behavior simply could not be overlooked. Therefore, after all other attempted solutions had served only to drive her into ever deeper isolation, there appeared to be one and only one solution to the needs of the grown-up girl, namely, the reverse dislocation into the comical phase. The changes in the diary of the group leader reflect the situation: "Becomes jealous of the little ones in the group"; "always bothers little girls particularly." Doris, however, had immediately sensed that the much desired reverse dislocation was impossible. This discrepancy triggered the *thrust.*

Presuppositions to the psychotherapy and its limitations

Such a conception of the thrust is not new nor are the psychotherapeutic suggestions that logically follow from it. The most impressive one was and still is the exemplary treatment described by Mrs. M. A. Séchehaye.[22,23] In somewhat simplified terms her magnificent method is explained as follows: The one-sided dislocation is confronted through the agency of a general "backward thrust," that is, the spontaneous regression is "therapeutically legalized" by means of a mother figure and thereupon, once the retrogression has been introduced, a new and "thrust-free" development is initiated.

The basic idea is, therefore, turning back time and thereby development too. Once that has been achieved, one should again start from the beginning, and this second effort should then be an improved one.

A comparable procedure would not have been advisable for the group leader in Doris's case for personal as well as for environmental reasons, because the framework of a school for deaf-mutes would by necessity have been disrupted by such an attempt. Furthermore, there is a significant factor that basically differentiates Doris's situation from that of Mrs. Séchehaye's patient Renée. In Renée's case a therapeutically nurtured regression was justified and promising because there was a distinct possibility that the young lady would, after a regression to an infantile level of development, reach a better and happier situation the second time. And Mrs. Séchehaye indeed was fortunately able to induce this development by means of her patience and goodness.

Doris's situation was a different one. In her we encountered that hard, nasty reality of deafness in combination with disfigurement. We could not evade this reality, certainly not by attempting a "new beginning," for sooner or later during the course of the therapy any procedure would have encountered this unavoidable fact: by no possible means could we improve matters a second time around. No matter how we might proceed, inevitably that nasty reality would have appeared with complete brutality. There had to be another way for Doris.

It became increasingly clear that it was less important to shield Doris in a motherly way than to help her to accept herself as she was and is. The path to self-acceptance could be found only by taking matters seriously. Taking things seriously is identical with discussion. I can take seriously only the person with whom I can discuss potentially or actually. At best I only pity the other kind of person.

Accordingly, the intensity of the discussions between Miss Hüberli and Doris was very valuable and promising. It was soon apparent that things were always much better when the teacher fought with the child, really fought with her (and this did happen from time to time), than when she pitied her.

For this reason the procedure Mrs. Séchehaye so impressively describes as *réalisation symbolique*[22] was inappropriate for treating Doris, because this method is completely devoid of discussion, in any case, discussion by the patient with his therapist. On the contrary, this method implies, indeed demands, an a priori unquestioning and unconditional attitude toward this unique psychotherapeutically treated patient, an attitude resulting from complete, unreflective identification with him.

To understand the extent of this consistent, thorough (and for the procedure of *réalisation symbolique* also completely unavoidable) partisanship, one needs to examine relevant passages in Mrs. Séchehaye's writing: all of the persons active in the drama, the girl's parents, the nurses in the hospital where Renée was treated, indeed even Renée's fellow patients, are observed and subsequently evaluated in an *absolute* sense, solely from the point of view as to whether and to what extent they were good for Renée. One cannot inquire about their actual individuality, indeed their specially formed need, in view of this partisanship, which cannot be set aside, and of the condition of identification when dealing with a single female patient.

It is superfluous to remark that the pioneering and exemplary procedure of the *réalisation symbolique,* which all psychotherapists who treat psychotics use in one way or another, would be incomprehensible in any form other than that described by its founder. It is probably just as apparent, however, that within the framework of a boarding-school a comparable procedure would not be permissible. Thus, we were at pains to demonstrate that the hopelessness of this procedure was not to be equated with inaccessibility for psychotherapy.

Discussion of the actual factors given and their influence

In a conversation with Mr. G. Ringli, the director of the school for deaf mutes, it occurred to us that perhaps we should attempt to reduce the child's disfigurement by cosmetic means insofar as it might be possible. We referred Doris to the dermatologist to get clarification as to whether it might at least be possible to eliminate the ugly synophrys of the growing together of the glabella and a part of the nose bridge by means of electrolysis of the brow roots. The result was negative; that procedure was said to be too circumstantial and might leave scars. In retrospect I am happy that from the start this procedure was completely ruled out. I am convinced that it would have been a mistake, even a dangerous one, for it would have restricted the child as well as us by limited, external measures, and would have prevented us from confronting a given situation with which we simply had to come to terms one way or another, namely, that of disfigurement, and would of necessity have discouraged us from facing up to the entire constellation immediately before us. It instead would have led to an unconditional appeal to that comfortable but pernicious easing of conscience that we had indeed tried everything possible but, because it was quite clear that nothing could be done, would not be compelled to do anything. Anyone frequently confronted with problems of this kind will have absolutely no doubt that even had the dermatologist or the plastic surgeon been able to make a substantial contribution to the improvement of Doris's facial disfigurement, her psychosis would have persisted. On the contrary, we would have been confronted with an identity crisis, in the original sense of that term, of great proportions. Thus, we could really have made things easy for ourselves by pointing out that the resulting situation was proof that we were simply facing a complex syndrome or even an endogenously conditioned development and its inevitable laws against which nothing could or should be done.

Now more than ever, no possible steps to improve the hearing, even if such steps gave promise of success (which was not the case with Doris), would have changed the sick condition of the child. The fact, substantiated by my own and my colleagues' experiences, leads to the following unavoidable, if also disillusioning conclusion: the disturbances of lived experience and conduct cannot be approached by way of "reality," and causal therapy is not the proper therapy for disturbed and lived experience.

Specific formation of the psychotherapy, conditioned by deafness and disfigurement

The unconditional confrontation

There was then from the beginning only one thing left to do, namely, to confront the entire situation directly, unconditionally, literally, that is, face to face. This I now did in the strictest sense of the term: I confronted Doris, face to face, my hands on her shoulders, permitting nothing at all to distract her or me. Doris was not prepared for this confrontation, a confrontation not *by* something, *with* something, but rather by *me* with *her*—and she behaved correspondingly. She reacted in an excited fashion and wanted to turn away. When she could not because I would not let her, she began to shout out inarticulate phrases in a loud, hoarse voice. I was able to grasp only scraps of her words, for most of what she shouted escaped me.

It should be noted that in her earlier healthy phases Doris, being almost totally deaf, spoke badly and with an unaesthetic articulation but was nevertheless understandable. In any case her speech presented no unusual difficulties for people accustomed to the speaking peculiarities of the deaf.

It is not unusual to hear the kind of inarticulate mumbling, such as that produced by Doris, by very excited deaf persons, by children more frequently than by adults, and indeed by those who in their good phases can command an understandable language. In this dramatic encounter with Doris it would have been impossible to reconstruct from her mutterings what she "might mean" on the basis of the scraps I could understand. Whatever she had to say, whatever she "wanted to" and "could" say, that she said even though her utterances were inarticulate, and every effort to derive something meaningful from them or even to confess the failure to understand and then ask what was meant would have proved to the child that it was no longer possible for her to relate. To persist in asking the meaning and significance of what she had said or even to attempt to abandon the direct confrontation and proceed to written communication would surely have resulted in the definitive collapse of the relationship.

From the very beginning then we ruled out any effort to ascertain accurately or to infer by means of questions or counterquestions what the inarticulate utterances were intended "to mean" or to state. After all, they were intended to mean only what they said and how they said it, even though the "words" were not understandable. Had Doris been willing to communicate differently from the way she did, had she been able to say words differently, then she would have done so.

In this situation there might have been the possibility of acting as though one had understood. But I believe that would not have been productive. "To act as though" has in psychotherapy always been a shortsighted lie and whoever deals with the deaf or with any patients in general who have a disturbance in relationship learns that an understanding is always limited even when the words are understood *as* words.

It was also possible to do something else in this situation, that is, to remain silent, a frequently tested means in psychiatry. Remaining silent is of course challenging and leaves everything open. Furthermore, in psychiatry the precept *si tacuisses* is more relevant than elsewhere, because in psychiatry one can by talking let one's tongue run away with one often and repeatedly. Earlier in similar situations with the deaf, I had often kept silent, at times even for long periods, not from embarrassment but, rather, intentionally in the belief and with the hope that in association with any human beings, including deaf persons, silence, that is, essentially presence, could become effective. However, my experience has emphasized for me that, contrary to what I had supposed, scarcely anywhere can silence be more deadly than in the presence of deaf people. It is less productive and more frightening only when one sits opposite a blind man, for the blind sink helplessly and hopelessly into oblivion in the presence of a silent person.[9]

Communication through echo

Accordingly I applied another principle with Doris, one attempted, tested, and used in various ways in connection with aroused deaf persons but also applied, occasionally with success, in relation to psychotics. I repeated exactly what I had perceived from various utterances of Doris, and I repeated it *precisely as* I had perceived it. What issued forth from me was just as unintelligible as what I had been able to perceive from Doris.[13]

It is difficult to describe in detail a "dialog" taking place in a direct face-to-face meeting, with one participant echoing whatever sounds the other made. The result was a peculiar yet genuine and quite intensive dialog which surely would have impressed a bystander not only as being utterly unintelligible but probably as being also burlesque. But there was nothing of the burlesque so far as the two partners in the discussion were concerned. Let me emphasize that anyone accustomed to this procedure can carry on this conversation through echoes with deaf people with great seriousness, reluctantly and anxiously to be sure, as I have frequently done even in the presence of my colleagues. It is probably superfluous to say that one ought to undertake the procedure only when one can give it the seriousness it deserves.

Sometimes in the course of such a dialog a better articulation is gradually achieved and thus one comes to understand later what the person had earlier intended. But that is not always the case and at the beginning of Doris's treatment we seldom attained that level.

Structuring of the therapy sessions

Doris and I, sometimes together, first walked over to a portable blackboard, always continuing our "talking together," this unconditionally consistent, direct, and incomparably intensive relating to one another, anything indirectly or only casually related being brushed aside. It usually happened that Doris would "draw me" and after she had completed her task with the chalk, we both distorted my likeness according to our whims, sometimes adding a beard or a big round belly.

We continued this procedure for weeks until the child found other means of expression. But even then we eventually returned to that drawing we did together on the blackboard as a reminder of our first conversations and their eventual conclusion.

The portrait of the doctor on the blackboard was at that time more or less true to life and, though his peculiar features were exaggerated, his portrait in that phase lacked any and all similarity to Doris's appearance.

Of her own accord Doris in that phase of the therapy never drew *herself,* and I would never have trusted myself to ask her to do so nor would I have had the courage to do it myself.

Rarely did I give Doris a piece of candy or anything like it. But on occasion Doris herself at the end of our session would come up from somewhere with a sticky, sweaty, little goody and hand it to me. I put it into my mouth even when it went against the grain to do so. I am of the opinion that one is more likely to be helpful to a child with Doris's affliction if one accepts something from her, particularly something edible, than if one offers the child something to eat; and this is particularly true in the case of a deformed, not to say repulsive child. Obviously Doris did not suffer because nothing had been given her: people gave to her but declined to receive anything from her.

Giving, and particularly the giving of food, leads all too easily to a full plate and, because of the situation, to a stuffing of the mouth. Descriptions of the treatment of appetent girls sometimes gives rise to the feeling that a person is being fed here, but while being fed is denied the right to complain or even to decline. But that is precisely what we do not want to achieve; we *want* Doris to complain!

These discussions with Doris never lasted very long, at most a half hour, sometimes even less. That is, to be sure, a short time. But the "therapy sessions" we have described were always extremely consuming and never allowed quieter moments to occur. The slightest indication of being weary would, in my judgment, have been very damaging to our relationship and to the further course of the therapy. Had I, even for a moment, shown distraction, then Doris would surely have relapsed again into her withdrawn attitude. It seemed to me better, therefore, to be refreshed for these sessions and to be completely with her all the time.

Frieda Fromm-Reichmann, and many others, in sessions

with psychotics had the same experience more than two decades ago, and she has convincingly defended the position that one cannot adhere to a rigid schedule in psychotherapy with psychotics.[15,16]

Primarily, however, this procedure was indicated not only for psychotherapeutic reasons but equally to economize time. Doris has on occasion been only one among a number of children who during the brief time allotted were undergoing treatment.

A brief remark regarding the local situation of the therapy: I usually saw Doris in the school for the deaf within the framework of the regular schedule, but when the treatment first began I also saw her at my home. At the beginning of the therapy we sometimes met three to four times a week.

For the discussions in the school, we took pains to see to it that whenever possible no single room and particularly no specially marked room was reserved for or declared to be a "doctor's office" or "therapy room." We met in any room that might just happen to be vacant and where we could remain undisturbed, such as a meeting room when the other children were outside, a classroom, sometimes even, heaven forbid, the teachers' room, or the bedroom shared by Doris with three other girls her age.

The basic principle was that the integration of the psychotherapy should be incorporated into the entire life of the school factually, indeed, in a purely topographical sense—for Doris as well as for the other children, and as completely as possible for the personnel. That idea and the objective of the psychotherapy were to be integrated and not separated. It is for that reason that to this very day I have no private office in the school nor do I want one.

The preceding paragraph refers to an experience resulting from a conversation with an English professional, Dr. Pierre Gorman, himself deaf. Years ago I told him of the simple conditions under which I practiced psychotherapy, and I owe it to him that I was able to make a virtue out of the necessity of the situation (and with a certain resentment: "not even a room of my own"). Today I regard the reservation of a special room in the school (and in the hospital) for the psychotherapist as not only superfluous but a harmful luxury, which happens also to lend support to the sequestration of psychotherapy.

The therapy proceeded in the manner I have described. We did not *talk to each other* or did so only occasionally, if for no other reason than that we had nothing to discuss with one another. Instead, when we did talk together, we in any case reached a mutual understanding, even though we did not have "language" at our disposal, nor were we disposed to language. During the therapeutic "dialog" I frequently understood, as at the beginning, only fragments of what Doris said.

While under therapy Doris gradually gave up her mutism toward the other children, her teacher, and the group leader, she retained her peculiarly inarticulate speech for weeks on end until the two of us commenced meeting. If I happened to see her in the company of the other children, we were able to speak together in completely intelligible language. In addition, however, she also retained a kind of "therapy jargon" which was limited to the therapy itself. I for my part occasionally accepted first bid by talking with Doris and then repeating what she had said, but I remained thoroughly uninterested as to whether or not I had been understood and equally uninterested as to whether or not I understood.

The structuring of the therapy in essence remained always the same. At first we talked to one another and subsequently we together undertook some project or other. I knew that Doris could not be dismissed, following our tense talking together, without a tension-relaxing return to the other children or to her classes. Later I shall discuss this principle of treatment and the basic considerations underlying it.

The course of the affection under psychotherapy

Behavior

The general behavior of the child, valued in terms of discipline, did not improve during that first phase of the therapy. Though Doris seemed more attentive, she also became annoying through manual activity. For weeks her "attentiveness" manifested itself only in its socially negative results. Her group leader writes: "Commences to annoy her fellow students and disturbs them in their work. For example, takes away the table cover when they are setting the table, so that they have to start all over again. This is pointless, however, unless it has been preceded by something else. One almost gets the impression that she enjoys doing things to spite the others. I [Hüberli] once take her forcibly from the dining room and tell her that she can do her work by herself when the others are finished. Becomes very angry, utters a loud cry and finally runs away. Hides herself in the most remote corner . . . cowers on the floor of the cold gymnasium like a pile of misery. . . ."

Doris's attitude toward the other children

We are no longer dealing with a purely resigned alienation. What is more important, however, is that Doris is able for the first time to give vent to her suffering. Miss Hüberli appends the following note to the report I have cited above: "When I am able after much persuasion to get her to talk, she tells me: 'All children are bad. I dislike all of them. They have strange faces. They are all from Italy.'"

Can anything express the tragedy of the situation more eloquently than the picture of the "strange faces" (illus. 1)

Illustration 1

that Doris drew at that time? After all, what is so strange about those faces? Nothing, absolutely nothing! Strange, of course, is the fact that the boys, Max, Hanspeter, Karl, and Werner, all of them classmates of Doris, are permitted to show their faces to the viewer while Doris, faceless, is turned away from him. Whereas the other children *have* faces, those faces are strange. Now, faces no matter how formed are strange. But Doris has no face at all. For the girl everything that is capable of being looked at, everything that "has" a face, is by that token evil. The child is incapable of meeting the glances of the others with her own face and glance. She is helpless and defenseless before them. Whoever experiences himself as unattractive—not to be looked at—is threatened by all who can look at him.

The shadowy form near Doris which, facing her, places its arm around the child is a later playful addition. It bears the features of the doctor and was added by Doris when we again, weeks later, took a look at the picture. One should not overrate this figure despite its fatherly bearing.

Illustration 2

The felt experience of the threat is manifested more clearly in the dream image in illustration 2 because the faces of the birds in their reductive schematism are more directly expressive of what the human faces implied in illustration 1.

56

The ducklings hopping about so good-naturedly in the center present a picture of contentment and of a closed community. Insofar as nothing moves outside of this foursome of little birds standing around together, the harmony is retained. Everything extraneous to that charming foursome remains a priori excluded. The little birds showing their faces to one another, albeit only their profiles are shown to the viewer, accept nothing into their circle. At the lower left near the border, in the foreground and close to the viewer, are the same characters, this time with their faces turned toward the viewer, however. The ears (quite properly for the deaf) are coordinated with the facial axis. But how different have these charming little animals become by means of this quarter turn! What "strange" faces they have now, suddenly, acquired! But strangest of all, more mysterious, and most threatening is the phenomenon standing in the upper part of the picture placed between the group of birds and the dreaming child, half hidden behind the window, seeing without permitting itself to be wholly seen, listening with large, pointed, indeed *literally pointed* ears, but not allowing itself to be audibly perceptible behind the closed window. The frighteningly mysterious thing about this anthropomorphic character, which by its schematism heightens the threatening nature of the disturbed relation almost to the point of being unbearable, is its presence in concealment. Relevant also is the fact that the eyes, which can hardly be seen, are capable of looking and, in addition, that the central point at which a person is viewed and at which he in turn localizes his own viewing function, that is, the area of the glabella, is covered by the window cross and consequently is invisible and thus incapable of relating. This strange character which from the very beginning keeps the viewer at a distance while it also excludes every other potential viewer stands guard by Doris's bed and thereby constitutes an inviolable *cordon sanitaire* about the child's sleep. Doris, to be sure, had written the notation "good" [*gut*] above the bed. The adverb "very" [*sehr*] was later added by me in conversation.

As Doris has especially emphasized, it is indeed good when one can be protected from faces, and this means being kept away from every conscious relationship, and from all inclination to relate. Only in that way, in complete isolation, can the child enjoy a good sleep. The unknown and unfamiliar are threatening and they result from everything that remains inaccessible to one's own choice and free will. And so this effect is made to appear in the picture by the showing of the face (by "showing oneself "); "hearing" has the same effect, a fact understandably represented by Doris as exposure of the ears.

It is interesting that the evil attributed to hearing as representing the differentness of the others finds expression only when Doris feels herself threatened by those who can hear. Only under such circumstances does she draw people or characters with visible ears (see illustration 14), whereas in the later phases of tranquility the ear motif disappears in the face-to-face representations.

In this drawing no kind of defense position against the unfamiliar has been erected. Indeed, the unfamiliar even stands guard over the child. Here not even the asseveration is completed, as it later is in illustrations 7 and 8. In the reproduction of this "good" dream the threat is still immediately there, and what keeps it at a distance has a disquieting identity with what should be kept away. The depth of the isolation, the extremity of the relational disturbance can probably not be demonstrated more tragically than by this casual, almost idyllic dream picture of the child pushed off into the upper left border of the drawing.

Briefly summarized, the tragedy of the situation can be described as "turning toward" or "facing a person" [*Zuwendung*] which in and of itself is identical with direct relationship, with encounter, and for Doris this has become identical with threat. The grade "good," which Doris gave the situation just described, therefore, means "good that I am removed from all relationship."

That relating is identical with conscious "turning toward" or "facing" holds true in general for all men, and also for animals insofar as conscious "turning toward" is possible for them. "Turning toward" for them means the turning of the face. For Doris, face to face with a healthy person, this fact has a double significance, however: first, because the girl is deaf and, second, because she is disfigured, moreover facially disfigured, so that a reciprocal irritation with the person standing opposite her results when both turn to face each other.

For the deafness, every turning away of the face, and therewith the possibility of reading articulated speech and the play of facial expression, means simply the identification with departure, with going away.

And for the facial disfigurement the situation is the following: the irritation of the other person, his possibly unconscious, unconceded, and therefore unadmitted rejection, constitutes a threat, which can only be evaded as the child anticipates the threat with a threat of her own.

Conscious relating, so we have determined, is identical with "facing" or "turning toward," indeed with reciprocal "turning toward" and "facing." Reciprocal facing, however, constitutes confrontation and, in some cases, conflict. Conflict means resolution and that distinguishes it from hatred. Doris's tragedy lay in the fact that resolution and conflict were no longer possible for her. She had recourse only to alienation or hatred. For Doris facing or "turning toward," as the dream-picture illustrates, signifies fright, as expressed by the two little birds in the foreground, or splendid isolation, as in the case of the watchful person in the window, which mysteriously obscures precisely those points at which

Doris is particularly stigmatized, namely, her nose, her eyes, and especially the area of the glabella (the locus of the ego). Doris herself is removed and alienated from everything.

Illustration 2 may bring home to us how traumatizing, yet healthfully traumatizing (so I had reason to believe), was the situatively conducted therapy which I had started with Doris. It was directly oriented toward a confrontation with the peculiar nature of the tragedy and the problems we encountered in the child's psychosis.

The experience of being looked at regarded as self-surrender

In the girl's complaints to her teacher we noted that she said all (strange faces) were *from Italy*. This remark has nothing to do with the current phobia, inspired by evil intent, which was being organized and exploited among certain segments of the Swiss population. The rejection of Italians was related instead to a certain experience; that the recollection of this experience should occur at this particular time is not particularly surprising. When Doris, during that phase preceding her psychosis, was provoking her fellow passengers on the train in a spiteful and malicious manner, her first encounter was with a passenger who came from Italy. This angry southerner gave public vent to his revulsion with corresponding temper and by means of mimicry rather than words, a fact that made him more intelligible to Doris. This Italian was presumably the first to confirm for the child what she needed to have confirmed, namely, that she was a repulsive, disgusting object whose behavior conformed to her appearance and who inspired aversion rather than sympathy.

Since that time the phrase "from Italy" connoted "arousing aversion" and therewith "being exposed," "naked, hopeless, and helpless, being destroyed by just being looked at," and this without one's being able to set the situation right or being able to evade it. The more clearly one becomes visible (and one becomes visible by being looked at), the more one is endangered. Therefore, to be looked at is identical with being destroyed, with being killed.

The foregoing is confirmed by two dreams of the child from that period: "The Italian is sitting in the train. A strange young lady is too. The latter had to undress, to undress completely. Later the two are in the bathroom and the man kills the young lady." Furthermore: "A young woman is asleep. She forgot to lock the window. A young fellow climbs through the window into the bedroom and holds a match to the young lady's eyes. The match burns— the young lady dies."

To be looked at means to be illuminated by glowing eyes. To illuminate is thus the same as to irradiate, to destroy with the rays of light which make everything visible and which kill. The child, carrying her disfigurement about with her and where she cannot hide it from others, must continuously experience her danger, based on her nakedness, as destruction.

Thus her facial disfigurement, especially that part of it around the eyes and particularly that centered between the eyes, implies of course a particularly perfidious kind of elementary relational disturbance. Disfigurement always brings about a feeling of endangerment. But the particular place on the body where this "Achilles heel" is located makes an enormous difference. The sooner I am able to dissociate myself from the location of the disfigurement, the sooner I can say "I *have* this or that" instead of "I *am* this or that" (all this of course presupposes the act of insight of which a twelve-year-old girl is utterly incapable), then the more capable I am of living with this affliction. The sooner I am, the more I am exposed. The more I have and hold, the more I find myself in a position to escape from the exposure. Every change in relation to the bodily norm makes having more difficult and increases the feeling of being exposed, and this condition becomes more exaggerated in proportion to the extent that the change can be observed.[10,12,13]

The manner in which such exposure is experienced has been portrayed by Dostoevski with an intensity that is lost on the casual reader, who usually fails to grasp what a decisive event has occurred.

In the course of the preliminary investigations connected with the charge of patricide against Mitya Karamazov, there is a physical examination. Mitya, self-conscious to the point of arrogance and absolutely sure of his innocence, even superior about the fact that they could not hurt or even importune his personality, has the following experience during the visitation with the investigating judge: "Something utterly unexpected and amazing to Mitya followed. He could never, even a minute before, have conceived that anyone could behave like that to him, to Dmitri Karamazov. . . . From pride and contempt, he submitted without a word." *

With the same pride and contempt he undressed before the official and finally took off his shirt and stood naked, yet all the while retaining his pride and his contempt for the sniveling official. "Mitya flushed red and flew into a rage. 'What, am I to stay naked?' he shouted. 'Don't disturb yourself. . . . We will arrange something. And meanwhile take off your socks!' " said the official.† As a final attempt at resistance the accused blurts out: " 'You're not joking? Is that really necessary?' Mitya does this with eyes flashing" (note, please, *with eyes flashing*). These very eyes were the ones which were to restrain the viewer from exposing the weak spot in the calm and aloofness of the investigation as ordered by the investigating officer. Whereupon the officer replied:

* Dostoevski, *The Brothers Karamazov*, trans. Constance Garnett (New York: The Modern Library, 1950), p. 585.
† Ibid., p. 587.

" 'Well, I must . . . ,' muttered Mitya and sitting down on the bed, he took off his socks. He felt unbearably awkward. All were clothed, while he was naked, and strange to say, when he was undressed he felt somehow guilty in their presence, and was almost ready to believe himself that he was inferior to them, and that now they had a perfect right to despise him. . . . 'It's like a dream, I've sometimes dreamed of being in such degrading positions.' "

Therewith the way was paved for the real humiliation, the high point of which is not the disrobing before all those clothed people but rather: "It was a misery to him to take off his socks." The reason for that becomes apparent, as is so often the case with Dostoevski, only incidentally. For his socks "were very dirty, and so were his underclothes, and now everyone could see it." *

This is the introduction: the painful admission that one is dirty, as it overwhelms many a person in the presence of his doctor and, above all, the accused, suspected of murder, in the presence of the judge.

But the really relevant specific is yet to come: "And what was worse, he disliked his feet. All his life he had thought both his big toes hideous. He particularly loathed the coarse, flat, crooked nail on the right one, and now they would all see it!" †

Now, shame—which is remarked in the novel—becomes overpowering, and indeed not only because of the deprivation, and not because of the uncovering of so-called regions

following little scene anticipates, long before the trial and before the struggle to determine the guilt or innocence of the accused, the end of Dmitri Karamazov:

* Ibid., p. 587.
† Ibid.

display of the marred physical parts. Following this, Dmitri is a broken man.

Illustration 4

But what a difference, what a significant difference there is between the physical situation of Dmitri Karamazov and our little Doris! Mitya *has* the deformed toes. He can look at them directly without the help of a mirror (a mirror can be deceptive anyway), can feel them, can become detached, and thus can come to terms with them and eventually fuse them into his body. Above all he can hide them arbitrarily. That, of course, is why the command of the investigating officer, which curbed this arbitrariness, was so humiliating. In short, whatever displeases Dmitri about himself he can accept or reject. In any case he can assume any attitude toward it that he wishes on the basis of his own decision. All this because of the common but all-too-often forgotten fact that we can imagine a human being who comes to us and says, "I" or "I

Illustration 13

Illustration 14

am" even when in addition there is something about him from which, because it is sufficiently removed from the point at which the I (the ego) is "located," he tries to sequestrate himself and is in a position to do so.

Thus three patients—the boy Max (according to Zulliger), Dmitri Karamazov, and our Doris—have presented us with three different kinds of noticeable bodily affliction. To attempt to understand Doris's uniqueness, the peculiarity of her relational disturbance, and the encounter with her, let us try to contrast the three types of affliction and their comparative effects.

All three patients reveal an affliction. In Max's case the affliction is always visible but in such a way that a withdrawal from it is possible both for the patient and for the person facing him. Max himself and his environment can imagine the boy apart from his affliction. Thus the a priori sympathy touches upon someone who has the affliction. Accordingly, Max can utilize what he has as an instrument. He is, therefore, able to evade an encounter with it.

Dmitri Karamazov related to his disturbance in a different way. *People* do not see it; nor does *he* see it. Not only can he evade it, he can even hide it or "suppress" it. Thus it is possible to say of him: "He disliked his feet." That is, he can care or not care about some part of himself. What he hides he does not come to terms with. By means of the provoked exposure before other people, particularly those wanting his guilt and shame and bent upon his incarceration, he is completely and unexpectedly exposed. Naturally he does nothing at all regarding the way *the others* react to his affliction. For him his affliction, his two big toes, stand between him and the others. He no longer has the affliction because he has hidden it. And now that it has suddenly bobbed up, he is expected to admit to something from which he had tried to separate himself.

In Doris's case the affliction is not only visible but one

Illustration 3

cannot look at Doris without also seeing it. To encounter a person visually means, in the last analysis, to view his face with your face. We do not really see each other when one of us turns his back to the other, as Doris presented it in illustration 1. A withdrawal by the afflicted party is impossible. There is more than this: Doris is unrepresentable without that part. She is identified with it. Indeed, she *is* her relational disturbance. A coming to terms without preparation is therefore not possible. It can be achieved only by a *juxtaposing* and confrontation.

With a glance Max can put those looking at him under a ban and thus embarrass them; thereby he becomes the a priori victor of the relational situation. Karamazov attempts something similar "with eyes flashing," but the affliction with which he never comes to grips, which he has hidden from the others as well as himself, is stronger than he is. He submits to it and therewith "everyone could see it." In Doris's case the glance is identical with the affliction. To be sure, there was a phase in which she sought to dominate the others by her glance; but this failed in a very miserable way. Thus there remained nothing for her but complete alienation. Hiding her affliction is identical with averting her gaze.

It may seem strange to compare three people so different in personality, training, and social situation. In fact, however, they do have points in common regardless of their differences. At the points common to them we may forget all psychology in the face of everything that relates directly or directly disturbs relating.

However grotesque it may sound, the extent of the suffering resulting from an affliction is in no way proportionate to the extent of the affliction itself; nor is there such a relationship between the extent of the affliction and the possibility of "controlling" that affliction.

We need to be aware of all this, if we want to understand the tragedy of Doris's situation. The little girl has not just one affliction; she is completely and at all times disturbed in her relational situation. The tragedy and problems of her situation are multiplied because Doris in her state of deafness and with her facial disfigurement cannot admit to anything; any utterance by her can achieve only a disturbed echo.

The X-ray examination as a specific agent

Had we come at the right time to the consideration I am about to describe, we would certainly have been able to shield the child against a severe trauma.

Precisely at the time Doris was filled with a general feeling of being threatened, a routine X-ray examination was being made of all the inmates of the school, of students as well as of personnel. For this procedure and its efficient conclusion a large conveyor with the X-ray apparatus accompanied by its personnel was moved into the school yard where the examination was conducted group by group.

Miss Hüberli gave the following report of Doris's reaction to this event: "Doris is scared and does not want to attend the examination. Speaks continuously about it, in general refuses to desist and permit her fears to be quieted. As the conveyance goes by our house, all of the children are still in the dining hall. Doris commences to cry loudly . . . also refuses to undress in front of the others . . . I therefore wait till the other girls are ready, but she continues to cry and uses her hands and feet to prevent being undressed. But finally she desists and allows me to undress her. Thereupon she is completely exhausted and listless as after a strenuous effort. Later on she insists on knowing whether everyone in the house was really X-rayed (she personally questions everybody), for she hopes to be able to prove to me that my statement that everyone was obligated to take the examination is not true."

The mobile X-ray laboratory was painted blue-white, the official colors of Zurich. But Doris "talked about a *red* auto and again queried everyone in the house, but none agreed with her, and though she was disappointed, she did not change her mind. She even made a corresponding drawing of the frightening car and dreamed about it."

In illustration 3 we find a representation of the dreadful vehicle. A look at it helps us to understand the terror it must have caused the girl. Does it not look as we imagine the gas extermination cars of Treblinka looked, fenced in and with an opening only for entering but not for leaving? No people are present. Destructive and inhuman technology alone is functioning here. Accordingly, this car cannot be blue and white; it has to be red, the color of the instrument which illuminates and irradiates everything and burns all things up in its fierce fire, exactly faithful to its prescribed function. Why and how should Doris let herself be convinced that something, for example this auto, looks *different* from what it *is* (after all *she* too is the way she looks)? The contradiction by the others regarding the color of the car can therefore (as the reporter noted) only be disappointing but not convincing.

Illustration 4 depicts what went on in the car. We see the child naked and exposed to the event. From behind, that is, from the place where one is fully exposed, the place from which it is impossible to encounter the face, there the rays radiate backwards on the defenseless girl. Her helplessly outstretched arm turned backwards is of no avail. Instead, it even emphasizes the exposure of the little girl standing before the wall and creating a flood of tears. The apparatus looks at the viewer with two round evil eyes. By means of them the machine transfixes the viewer, distracts his gaze and therewith his participation from the child, and leaves her to flounder before this demonic pair of eyes. Thus Doris's isolation is complete. If the viewer is transfixed by the gaze of the apparatus, then the latter, undisturbed, can do with the child whatever it pleases. Illumination [AN-leuchten] and irradiation [DURCH-leuchten] are one and the same, just as

Illustration 16

Illustration 10

when a healthy person can understand and react to a glance, unavoidably directed toward him, as a "penetrating" look. How much more meaning and truth must this look have for that facially disfigured girl. Had she been fully undressed, that would have made no difference to her feeling of exposure as opposed to the condition in which Doris pictured herself, that is, her "shame" which is in her face and not in the "shame-locus" [pubic region].

In Doris's representation of the chest examination in illustration 4, we find still another highly instructive detail. The fluorophotograph of the child, signed with her right name,* hangs far away in the upper left corner. It corresponds completely to X-ray schematism, hence is grasped objectively. However, there is no relationship between the dreadful scene the child experienced in the toils of the X-ray and the fluoroscope and the innocently objective X-ray picture projected at a distance. The schematized X-ray shows clearly that the children of the institute had been properly and thoroughly instructed, prior to the examination, about the conduct, meaning, and purpose of the X-ray clarification, but that for Doris who had all the same instructions the purpose was far removed from her grasp. The gap between every explanation and the felt experience of reality can be demonstrated with graphic clarity. Is the situation any different in other situations requiring explanation, for example, in sex education?

It would be meaningless and insincere if after the fact we tried to find a justification for our having exposed Doris to this severe trauma. Had we at the time understood what we now think we do, we would certainly have excused the child from the fluoroscope examination. But we did not, and so there remained only the attempt of acknowledging our mistake and, if possible, of proceeding from the mistake to

* For the purpose of medical secrecy, the name was covered before our reproduction was made, and so is not visible in illustration 4.

something more constructive, such as declaring our willingness to assume all responsibility for the consequences that had been so harmful to the child.

In general, this minor result, derived from a scene intrinsically meaningless (that is, the fluoroscope examination) which, "objectively" considered, is not dangerous, illustrates once more how very important it is to ascertain the specificity of the so-called trauma. Indeed, because the trauma need not have a "traumatic" effect, we might better refer to it as an agent.[4] The realization of the "excessiveness," that is, the "severity" of the trauma, for which we do not have valid indices, provides no understanding as to why, when, and to what a psychotic reaction occurs. We must, on the contrary, confess that the gradation and evaluation of the trauma are not only not helpful but extremely harmful, because they seem to accord the person doing the gradation the competence to determine when something is "empathic" and when not and, therefore, to determine which pathological stance is "proper" or "improper." In this way the outsider easily becomes the judge who ascertains by what "severe degree" and onward, a trauma must be regarded as "sufficiently bad." By such procedure and its consequences, however, we must conclude that the willingness to dispense with the coming to terms with a situation leads to the end of the psychotherapeutic stance.

Transition from rejection to dependence

Following this episode, which could not possibly have occurred at a less favorable time than during the phase when the child was beginning to come to terms with her environment, the attitude of the girl changed again. Doris now became depressed.

This condition by itself and viewed against the entire development can be regarded as neither favorable nor unfavorable. One's own attitude toward it determines whether the depressed behavior marks the beginning of lethargy and thus an unhealthy development or whether it marks the assumption of the patient's coming to terms with himself, and thus the beginning of convalescence. The depressed phase, which occurs after (indeed, in my experience, regularly follows) an initial psychotic condition, depending upon whether it has been taken into account and fused into the therapy or whether it has been overlooked or simply been relegated to medication (the worst possible alternative), has a favorable or a ravaging effect on the entire course of the illness, that is, of its prognosis.[5] We have therefore devoted much attention to this important phase.

"Complains and moans continuously," writes Miss Hüberli, and adds, "which was formerly not the case. Lets herself go to pieces, lies down on the bed in her clothes, later on the floor of the bathroom." Notes about the forwardness of the child follow. During this transition from rejection to dependence the child must under no circumstances be disillusioned. Miss Hüberli recognized the appeal without further consideration. She notes: "I put her to bed like a little baby."

The relation of the girl is restricted for the moment to her teacher and to the doctor. In every other respect she remains isolated. "In school she achieves little, indeed only what is sternly demanded. Her former eagerness to learn and the satisfaction derived from it are lacking." I believe that the additional observation of Miss Hüberli is correct: "But yet she needs this rigid ordering and submits to the stern discipline of the teacher." Both of the two stances, the helpful, protective, and permissive one as well as the stern, unambiguous one, would be wrong, if one tried to play them off against each other. Accordingly we try to give each its chance in its own due time. The magnificent attitude of both parties is extremely helpful, as is the combination of their readiness to justify their actions and of the preservation of

Illustration 7

Illustration 9

the spontaneity of the teacher, a spontaneity free of all psychology. In the notes we read: "In her free time . . . she does not know what to do with herself and therefore continually asks, what shall I do?" At the time I advised Miss Hüberli not to "restrict" Doris during her free time. This lack of restraint had the following consequence: "First off, she sits motionless on a chair for two hours and stares straight ahead . . . later she runs over to me, sits down beside me and lays her head on my lap. (She has been acting this way quite often of late.) Her attachment and need of affection grow greater and greater." Thus the teacher could persuade herself to regard forwardness as attachment but not without resistance and reservations, many of which were justified and compelling, for example, "But amidst the other eleven [*sic!*] children I cannot and will not pay undue attention to her wishes." The consequences of the necessarily ensuing frustration are unavoidable: "If I send her away or pay her no attention, she gives me disciplinary difficulties, creates disturbances wherever she can. . . ."

One has to ask whether it would not have been advisable in this—doubtless very decisive—situation to assign some special person exclusively to care for Doris, or to release Miss Hüberli from most of the responsibilities for her large group, so that she could devote herself fully to Doris with all the intensity and sacrifice required, something she had been unable to do because of the prevailing conditions and for temporal reasons as well as pedagogical. However, this we did *not* do. Our negative decision was based on the reflection that any such action would serve only to isolate the child still further from her group to which she had remained attached to a remarkable degree. Her group leader notes: "The other children in the group continue to help her and look after her. The way Doris is borne by the whole group is quite remarkable." It seemed to me then as it still does now, that the danger of *isolation* is greater and more persistently

Illustration 11

harmful for a child like Doris than the danger of *frustration*, conditioned as it would be by the human and temporal demands on the teacher, even if this frustration were difficult and disturbing for the time being.

The cure was supposed to proceed as "naturally" as possible and within the framework of the operations of the school, though with "a minimum" of interference from the latter. This was the basic principle. It was applicable to the presence of the girl in her group and to her position in the school as well as to the relation of the group leader to her. Repeatedly I warned Miss Hüberli never to undertake anything with Doris which she felt forced to do—and no matter how convincingly I explained to her why I believed that it was desirable to do this and to desist from doing that—she had also to remain silent about anything that did not seem natural to her or to which she could not whole-heartedly subscribe.

Simple suggestions frequently served to bring about seemingly insignificant yet essential turns or changes: for example, "I shall try to follow the advice of the doctor 'to hold Doris before letting her cling to me.'" We recall how detrimental to the feeling of freedom, how very disturbing almost to the point of nausea but also how injurious to their relationship, to their mutual empathy, did that severe cling-ing by Doris seem at times to her teacher. Thus, however, by means of this irrelevant reversal of roles and only by this means—that the teacher did the holding instead of letting herself be held—did Doris change from a captive to a free person who, by embracing instead of by having to cling, preserves her activity and can feel free in the knowledge that she is able at any time to relax this active embracing. A short passage reveals the lessening of the embarrassment the teacher formerly experienced: "I (Hüberli) seemingly unin-tentionally put my hand on her knee. Doris remains quiet and motionless for a while without embracing me. When I take away my hand, she quickly pulls it back and says: 'No. Please keep it there.' Then suddenly talks about her home. . . ."

We must not be surprised that in this little scene Doris did not see an activity satisfying to her teacher but rather only an invitation to demand more, that is: "One evening she is more restless than during the last several days. She comes and asks whether she might sleep in my bed. This thought just happened to occur to her and will not leave her. Begs and implores and refuses to settle down till I finally close my door. At eleven o'clock she gives up and excuses herself."

Transition from dependence to reciprocity

With good reason the majority of child psychotherapists might well have advised the group leader, and particularly in that decisively important phase, to undertake a more active and permissive procedure. Some might even regard it as a professional mistake that I did not tell Miss Hüberli how helpful it might have been, under the circumstances, had she taken the child into her room and even into her bed. However, I desisted from all that and even declined to query Miss Hüberli about what deterred her from taking Doris into her bed. Questions of this kind, regardless of their emphasis, are always understood as including the suggestion "actually you should have done that!" I limited myself to listening to the group leader about her difficulties with the child. By referring to certain little scenes excerpted from her reports Miss Hüberli was able to realize how close the girl had become to her. So close, indeed, that one could suggest that she might give Doris a doll.

But Miss Hüberli did not just buy her any old doll from a store. Instead she gave her little "Ditti," which she herself had had for some time and was personally dear to her, and which Doris frequently had seen lying on her teacher's couch. When Miss Hüberli decided to take this action, the moment was indeed ripe for it. Now Doris truly could rightfully feel that her teacher was presenting her with something of herself and that she had not merely performed a formal ritualistic act, perhaps only to buy herself free from actual engagement.

This situation did not develop, however, until two days after the scene by the bedroom, already described. First, Miss Hüberli had to allay her doubts about whether to give the girl something, that is, to share her motherly nest, something she was not prepared to do. To encourage Miss Hüberli to share her nest with Doris would have been no less a demand than the one that the princess give up half of her bed to the king of the frogs. I believe, therefore, that the spontaneous gift of the doll was better and more wholesome, because the intent was more sincere, than some other kind of compelling and compulsive and revolting act, even if the latter had been accompanied by a more meaningful attitude. "I am going to follow the doctor's advice and tomorrow evening give her a doll with my name. Doris accepts it gladly and is quite content with it."

That the timing of the action was right becomes apparent from Miss Hüberli's note, immediately following: "After a week she apparently has no further need of the doll and so she gives it back to me." In my view Doris by returning the doll indicated precisely that she understood what and how much her teacher had given her by means of this little doll, that she, Doris, not only could receive but could also give, and thus that she was being taken seriously. And I am convinced that to be taken seriously is more important for a child like Doris than being taken care of. I cannot emphasize sufficiently how important the principle of reciprocity is in the psychotherapy of all forms of elementary relational disturbance whether it takes place in the area of coming to terms with one's self or, as here, in gift and counter-gift. On the contrary, one-sidedness is more injurious than denial (refusal).

Up to this point I had refrained from giving Doris anything. Only following the reciprocal action with the teacher could I give the girl a little present—it just happened to be Christmas. A drawing (illustration 5) documents this scene but also reveals something else, namely, that Doris is not merely a recipient. On the same day she indicated her intention to give me a clothes brush, nicely decorated by her some time ago. Once again something had occurred on both sides.

Illustration 5

Doris and I are facing each other in illustration 5 and related to each other by means of the exchange of gifts. But both of us are mere skeletons and not real figures. Our faces resemble each other just as one skeleton drawing resembles

Illustration 6

another. Nothing specific relative to Doris or to me is in the picture. But one might regard it as a promising item that in the picture I am taking a step toward the girl.

The foregoing has relevance for the situation in illustration 6, because if one recalls the long-standing significance for Doris of St. Nicholas as the real bogeyman, that is, as a threatening spirit, then one might enjoy with some satisfaction looking at his present appearance. But one should not overrate the assertive power of this drawing. Santa Claus, formerly the bogeyman, looks quite good-natured. But he is a very impersonal character who walks into the forest past the viewer without any real relationship whatever to him. The sickly portrait of human beings has not yet changed in any decisive way; it has only become more tolerable for the moment as a result of "impersonalization" and therewith is highly suspect from the psychotherapeutic point of view; on the whole it is actually sicker than during the time of severe threat. The drawing is evidence of a pseudocure, which could put one at ease prematurely. Everything in the picture looks so quiet and peaceful. But the peace we encounter here is an impersonal, resigned, and therefore a false peace. Such a peace would be conceivable as the result of psychopharmaceutical treatment; indeed, it might be regarded as the most favorable consequence of that kind of essentially leveling therapy.

The stage of challenge

The actual situation of the girl, characterized as it was both before and after by a quite remarkable calmness which was really self-isolation and withdrawal, did indeed correspond to the foregoing. Inasmuch as this phase threatened to become habitual, I undertook to approach Doris on the grounds of her differentness. On such occasions one seldom hits upon the right words, particularly in the presence of a deaf girl. I no longer remember what I said in particular except for one sentence, "You are different from the other children, yet we are fond of you." And then for the first and probably the only time during the therapy I stroked her head.

In consequence of this approach Doris rejected me for several days. "I do not want to go to the doctor" . . . and pretended to have a "severe stomachache," according to Miss Hüberli's notes. I, however, said the same thing to her a second time.

The recollected alienation

The following night she had a dream, of which she also immediately made a drawing (illustration 7). Over and over again she declared spontaneously, "That is my first really good dream." It was about a football game. I have forgotten what actually took place. In any case we see the child in a calm state, but also being advised to be calm by her teacher, standing at some distance in the doorway. However, Miss Hüberli though at a distance is also much nearer by virtue of her alter ego in the form of the doll which Doris has in bed with her.

But what then is so good about this dream? Nothing really except one thing, that at the very least this dream, though it does not reflect daily life, ultimately reveals to Doris the depiction of her actual life, that is, she is not participating in the football game but, instead, is lying there by herself alienated by means of the bedspread from her environment. Not even as an event can the dream create relationship between Doris and the world around her! The dream itself is still split off. Closely encapsulated in a blister, impenetrable from all sides except for a narrow opening toward Doris, it remains firmly closed to everything outside. The events of the dream exclude even Miss Hüberli and even the doll representative of her. In short, no relationship between Doris and others is formulated even in the dream.

However, the drawing also reveals against what the child, together with her dream, must alienate herself: the ceiling light, locked into a protective grid and thus isolated from the sleeping child so that it cannot illuminate the girl and show the others what she looks like. Even stranger and more frightening is what approaches the child from above on the left and which compels the dream, isolated in the blister, to make way lest it be run through by it; this is the pealing *sound* that penetrates through the open window, for the open window as a pealing sound represents that penetrating hostility from which the dream is forced to retreat. (After all, light would be able to penetrate the window even if it were closed.) This little perception discloses a peculiarity which we often encounter and misconstrue in our efforts to gain basic insight into what deafness really is and how it is experienced, namely, that a person with hearing loss, the deaf person, is usually assumed to have lost the world of sound. And from this assumption many theorems and psychological concepts have been derived. But this one little drawing of Doris's dream suffices to convince us how inapplicable this common assumption is, for the pealing sound is not nonexistent for Doris. It is there though insufficiently integrated. Because it can be perceived, however, though not properly integrated and not adequately mastered by means of sound remnants and vibrations, particularly in the cutaneous system, pealing sound constitutes a threat to the deaf child. (Incidentally, this threatening effect is stronger in the child who is hard of hearing than in the deaf child.) Thus, the tragedy of deafness lies in one's being exposed to sound and not to "the absence of the world of sound."

To repeat, the frightening and irritating misfortune for deafness is that a deaf person cannot integrate sound, that he can "make no sense" out of it, that *he* does not control sound but rather that sound controls *him,* and that it can "do what it will" with him.*

* This corresponds to the observation of my colleague, Elizabeth Kronauer, that deaf persons are much more afraid of noise than are those who can hear.

Isolation results from these effects and doubly so for Doris, for she because of her disfigurement feels the need to be isolated not only from sound but also from light.

The differing manner of the isolation, namely, from the light coming from above, on the one hand, and, on the other, from the sound penetrating from the outside, adequately demonstrates the differing manner by which the visual and auditory relational elements are experienced. Doris is able to exclude the light by putting a protective grid around the light. To the sound, however, she is fully exposed, for it is ubiquitous and penetrates everything. Accordingly, *she feels compelled,* because she is unable to eliminate sound, *to isolate* (that is, alienate) *herself from it.*

What Doris has drawn applies not only to persons afflicted with relational problems but to everyone else. Only a deaf child, however, would be able to portray in a convincing and simple fashion this generally applicable situation of the experiencing of light and sound. She needed the ability, to be sure, to isolate herself, an ability not yet available in the dream of illustration 2, in order to demonstrate what is required if one wants to cope successfully with the threatening elements.

When I look at this kind of picture, I fail to understand why there are so many people who want to argue emphatically and even carry on a controversy against the concept of "splitting." In my view this kind of activity is based on a decisive misunderstanding regarding what occurs in splitting. One simply cannot asssume by oversimplification that splitting [*Spaltung*] has something to do with "being split" [*Zerspaltensein*] or "becoming split" [*Zerspaltenwerden*], a view comparable to the Old Swabian joke (from a poem by Gustav Schwab):

> Zur Rechten sieht man wie zur Linken
> Einen halben Türken herunter sinken.

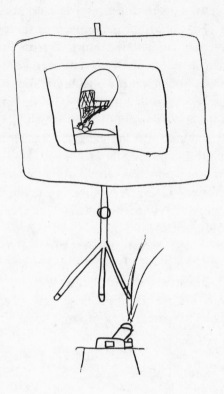

Illustration 8

To the right as well as to the left
One sees half a Turk falling down.

The situation is not that simple. Illustration 7, however, demonstrates clearly what does occur in the process of splitting, and we can realize from the picture that splitting off is a real and demonstrable occurrence. Indeed, we actually see this occurrence (not "isolatedness," for there is no such thing, but instead "being split off" [*Ab-spalten*]) spontaneously and unambiguously recorded by a child.

The primitive and popular notion, which also unfortunately prevails in some professional circles, that everything which the word "splitting" [*Spaltung*] may connote, be it in German or in the customary Greek designation, must be interpreted as "division" [*Zerteilung*], has great suggestive power, and thus harbors within itself the danger that those who operate with the word may succumb to its implications. It is well to remember that the creator of the concept schizophrenia held firmly to the view that in dealing with schizophrenia one is dealing with "splitting off." Thus did Eugen Bleuler in his original monograph on schizophrenia literally speak of the "isolation (or splitting off) of individual groupings of imagination or of conation." [3b]

Once more we are enabled by means of the situation of elementary relational disturbance to understand thoroughly and with graphic clarity, indeed paradigmatically, that is, as presenting an example for the common situation of mankind, what actually can be observed as occurring in isolation.

The dream occupies Doris for a very long time. She draws it over and over again and with ever stronger reductions of motif. From this kind of development and reworking we learn increasingly more about the actual meaning and the angular turn the dream had for the child. All this is apparent in the variation of the dream presented in illustration 8. Nothing tangible remains of the football game. All persons, even Miss Hüberli and the doll, have disappeared. What remains much changed and in much sharper perspective is the isolation. Not only the dream but also the dreamer are again and even doubly enclosed by a frame (isolated in the frame). The elimination of light is achieved by projecting the entire event as a photograph. Inasmuch as the scene appears in a projection, the isolation is convincing and "literally" objective, that is, demonstrable by means of the objective.

If we compare this dream with the one Doris reproduced for us in illustration 2, we are able to understand how she could regard the dream as the first good one she had ever had. All this not *although,* but rather *because* in it the tragedy and nature of isolation appeal to us much more directly and evidently than in that other dream with the birds.

The realization of being different

The picturing of her own situation which led to the coming to terms with herself quite naturally made the girl unhappy at first. Doris no longer carries on about her disfigurement as she had done in such a challenging way during the second phase; nor does she obscure her disfigurement and thereby herself as she did in the subsequent phase. Instead, she now directs her attention to it. At first she seeks refuge in procrastinations. For weeks, for example, she fusses around about her clothes as though they were the factor that determined her appearance and that therefore through them she could also affect her disfigurement. We encounter the following notation: "She becomes critical regarding her dresses (until now she had been indifferent and wore many dresses given to her here and was pleased with them). All that suddenly stops. She now wants to wear only what pleases her. But also in this respect everything occurs in such an extreme way that once I had to leave her at home crying and raging after we had been invited to attend the theater because she no longer wanted to wear her winter coat. And even when all the other girls say that the coat is pretty and one of the girls even wears one just like it, the coat is no longer pretty to Doris."

But this evasion by means of clothing remains possible for only a short time. The therapy with its continuing confrontation would not permit this to continue. Soon thereafter Miss Hüberli notes: "Her appearance is indeed causing her concern. She suffers from the fact that her eyes vary in color and that she has a grey lock of hair. Why do I have these things, she often asks and complains about the fact that the children sometimes stare at her so. . . . In the train she also often has the feeling of being looked at." All this despite the fact that for several preceding weeks she had conducted herself in such a way that people *were compelled* to stare at her!

"After a visit with Dr. B. she says to me [Hüberli]: 'That boy of a doctor has a nice face, long, narrow. I believe he is intelligent.' " In this phase Doris is capable of uttering the question: "Why do I have that?" She is no longer just different from the other children. She is able to compare herself to the others even to her own disadvantage. But it sounds like resignation. Indeed, her statements sound as unenvious as only resigned statements can. "Why do I have that?" is now the question. As yet there is nothing challenging, such as there might be in the question, "Why does the boy not have that?" or more directly in the question, "Why do *you* not have that?" which she could direct to the other person.

The desperate situation and Doris's mastery of it

In this moment of complete, resigned realization of the unalterable state of differentness we probably reached not only the most desperate stage of the therapy but also the most desperate situation generally in which a therapist might find himself with his patient. How pertinently such a therapist might cite at this point in a more or less sarcastic manner, and if not sarcastic then ever so hopelessly, the limits of all efforts to influence or help! Over and against the sinister *reality*, namely, the disfigurement of the child combined with her deafness, all psychotherapy seemed to reveal its inadequacy. And so one could in all seriousness ask one's self whether the achievements to date, that is, the coming to terms with the relational disturbance instead of, as previously, the agitation by means of it or the attempt to obscure it, were not much worse than the prior condition. What possible good could yet accrue from such a situation?

But Doris herself knew better and there was nothing left for us to do except to declare ourselves amenable to her better knowledge. For in this phase another dream occurred and the events in the dream took place, according to Doris's own account, as follows: "Dream about the Eskimos: We are flying to Lapland. Miss Hüberli, Miss . . . [all of the school's group leaders] are Eskimos. The Eskimos are having fun. The child Eskimo cannot catch any fish. She is clever. She gets a big knife. She cuts into the ice with the knife. She makes a circle. Suddenly she falls into the water. The Eskimo mother comes to the aid of the child. She dries the child. The man Eskimo catches a fish. There are many fish in the basket. Miss Hüberli and Miss B. cook the fish. Miss Z. and Miss G. set the table on the ground. It is cold. Suddenly a ship approaches. Miss Hüberli, Miss . . . ride away on the ship."

For days thereafter Doris called me Eskimo. We saw each other only infrequently at that time and had no opportunity to discuss this motif. And so I had no notion of what it meant.

One day later I again received a long letter from Doris. On a large sheet it contained an account of the Eskimo dream and beneath it a second dream entitled "About China," as follows:

"Miss Hüberli and I fly to China. Suddenly I fall asleep. Miss Hüberli wakens me. China* are having fun. Miss Hüberli looks at many houses. The child fetches me. The child says, you may also play. I say, what? The child says, catch. Suddenly a funny clown appears. The clown plays in the bubble bath. He blows the bubbles to me. Suddenly my face is dirty. Miss Hüberli washes my face. We fly to Zurich. The China are sad."

* The use of "China" throughout is as Doris transcribed it.

The lower half of the enormous page is occupied by two full portraits. One is called Eskimo, the other China (illustration 9).

The day after I had received the long letter from Doris we encountered each other again but had little opportunity to talk about this dream. I said to her only: "I am glad, Doris, that you have come back to us again from China."

For the moment nothing much remained to be added about that. Thereupon much occurred directly and of its own volition. Finally and for the first time *Doris had portrayed herself just as she is.* How did that come about? First the Eskimo had appeared groping, reserved, uncertain, cool, and remote in the cold country, but then came the female inhabitant of warm China, deciduated yet colorful, pleasant, and cheerful! The two drawings document all this: the colorless pencil sketch of the Eskimo (not reproduced here) reflecting uncertainty, and the clear, warm, pastel colored representation of the contented Chinese (illustration 9).

But the two dreams actually show all this even more clearly, for they reveal the recognition of her own peculiar character and especially of her form. (We note that the dreams resemble each other markedly as regards motifs, though the second dream is a more unambiguous and intensive recasting of the first.) By means of the dreams Doris has now found the path to those who look like her and consequently *are* just like her. Now she is no longer alone and is no different from the others. In the first dream her identification with the Eskimos, particularly her stance toward the child Eskimo, still remains unclear and only hinted at. Even the initiation, that is, the baptism, probably the nucleus of both dreams, still fails to reveal the character of the identification unambiguously. In the Eskimo dream the identification occurs "by accident," for the cunning child Eskimo herself must first anticipate the requirements which cause her to fall into the water. Even at this point the identification of Doris with the child Eskimo remains ambiguous. And the question also remains open in the dream whether she gets the fish the Eskimo man brings and which Miss Hüberli fries. Finally, however, all appear to have gone, the teachers as well as the Eskimos. It is cold and Doris alone stays behind. Finding their way to each other has, alas, vanished just as the dream has.

But the China dream provides the decisive breakthrough. The first dream is obviously incapable of achieving this. A *double dream*, a twofold narcosis, is required to effect the deposition of the encroaching event, such as the sleeping in the dream, which is an occurrence we sometimes encounter whenever a dream indicates or even initiates basic shift.

Thus doubly secluded and protected, the child journeys to distant, warm China. There at first she no longer requires her teacher. For she is now among her own, among trusted friends, and all of the Chinese are happy that one of their own has come to them from afar.

This event must moreover be "symbolically" confirmed and emphasized and thereby validated beyond the immediate present. This occurs in the rite of "baptism." And this time the baptism as a Mongolian* takes place unambiguously.

Its completion is no longer associated with accident. Doris does not fall into the water because of clumsiness on her part, as happened in the Eskimo dream, nor does she first cleverly have to simulate this fate.

An appointed baptist, "a merry clown," now appears on the scene, the extraordinary transformation of her own foreign, different essence, burlesque and yet a bit sinister as is everything "merry" relative to its assigned task, to complete

---

* It hardly requires mentioning that the fact we are not dealing with actual mongolism has any significance for Doris. As we pointed out earlier, the antimongolistic placement of the eyes actually has a much more mongolistic effect than the syndrome usually associated with that term.

the act. "He blows soap bubbles toward me." But her face gets dirty from the soap bubbles as though it first had to disguise itself until it got washed by the teacher and thereby becomes a Chinese face visible to everyone. The man himself now has another role toward Doris. He no longer provides her with food but instead initiates her.

Scarcely has the decisive act been completed, scarcely has the girl been welcomed into the fold of her own kind, scarcely has it thus been determined that she is at home somewhere, then she has to leave this newly found home and return to her real home. "The China are sad." Doris says nothing about her own feelings. And precisely this end to the dream, the fact that Doris has to leave the place where her kind are at home, makes it possible for her, indeed compels her to recognize her true nature in all its peculiarity. For had Doris remained in China and thus become an inhabitant of an imaginary foreign land, then the Chinese would have had no reason to be sad. But in that case the decisive event would not have occurred, for the isolation would not have been dissolved! In view of the present situation Doris became the self-conscious representative of a people residing on this earth even though far away, a representative not among her own people, for there is nothing to represent among one's own, but rather among another people, a people *recognized by her.* After that dream the child decorated the canopy above her bed with many pictures of Chinese people.

Henceforth Doris experienced herself. Like every other experiencing of self, this one also took place in a responsive way. But what up to the present was never possible—to experience herself in her being and in her particular self from and by means of the answer given from without—now became successful through the medium of the dream. The others here are not Chinese. She, however, is a Chinese, and there are, indeed, Chinese in this world even though they live far away. The child is in no way concerned about whether and to what extent we are dealing with a dream or with "reality." *

Naturally, this situation offers only a temporary solution of the problem, but we must be pleased and acknowledge it. And indeed we are. We share Doris's joy or at least we seek to do so insofar as that is possible. And finally, together with a remarkable improvement in the child's disposition, we begin to realize some corroboration of this solution to the problem we once feared was not even to be thought of, indeed seemed to be nonexistent.

Doris's new situation is delightfully represented in illustration 10. Various persons around Doris have now become like her, that is, have become Chinese. Everything, the landscape as well as her school, has gone to China. Miss Hüberli, the Chinese mother, carries Doris, the little Chinese girl, around on her back according to Chinese custom. The doctor, though somewhat removed, watches the two of them approvingly from the terrace like a good-natured mandarin. Isolation can be observed neither in the picture nor in general from this point on. For weeks everything in the pictures spontaneously drawn by the child remains Chinese. Even the Christ child and the angel accompanying the Holy Family in flight to Egypt, all these are Chinese (illustration 11).† The little boy also—as far as the motif and execution go—does not represent an original creation of Doris's imagination but a copy taken from the picture book *Le Ballon rouge* [*The Red Balloon*] (illustration 12).

One might assume that this manner of representing

---

* In view of the central position of the dream of the Chinese in the child's evolution we should add something about the role and the stance of the clown. Viewed historically, the figure of the clown developed from the representation of death in medieval mystery plays. Today it is that extraordinary character which artfully disfigures itself to reveal to people the truth of their anxiety while making them laugh. In the dream the clown assumes the role of the comical little Doris. During the following day something similar occurred: I stressed the clown in the presence of Doris, so that she would no longer have to create him!

† This phase of Doris's treatment happened to take place during the Advent period.

herself and her world as "Chinese" derived from some innate peculiarity of Doris. But that is not the case. China is an entirely new discovery by her. Several earlier drawings executed during the pre-psychotic phase will document how very differently, indeed how diametrically differently, Doris experienced the world at that time. The fat carp, sailing so contentedly through his element (illustration 13), has nothing "Chinese" about him. But even more impressive, because it is actually "anti-Chinese" in a pronounced way and for that reason indicative of how distressed, isolated, and threatened its creator felt, is illustration 14 which Doris drew just prior to the onset of her psychosis. Four very round eyes stare at the girl. These four eyes belong to persons having radically different kinds of eyes, who represent a unity together and are well hidden from the girl, who will never be one of them. These eyes signify only the accentuation of her loneliness and the threat through all other eyes. The fact that the eyes are patently those of the great horned owl, the only bird with visible hearing organs that determine its physiognomy, also accentuates the situation of feeling threatened, which speaks forth so eloquently from the drawing by this disfigured deaf child (illustration 14).

Perhaps the lost little young bird above and to the left in the nest contains a hint of something "chinese." This bird appears in illustration 15, drawn just prior to the psychotic disturbance; in the company of its mother it is chirping in the wrong direction, the direction from which nothing, certainly neither protection nor food, is to be expected.

When and if we let the pictures Doris drew or painted pass in review before our eyes as a series, they cause us to reflect very seriously on the danger associated with every kind of expression therapy, be it with children or adults. Aesthetic criteria must never be applied in the attempt to evaluate expressive achievements in psychotherapy. Unfortunately this kind of contamination in the evaluation of the

Illustration 12

patient's degree of improvement through considerations of artistic achievement affect the therapist more easily than he would like to admit to himself. Doris's series of pictures leave little doubt that the ones she created before her manifested psychosis (illustrations 13–15) are much richer, more colorful, more self-willed, and artistically more appealing than those done during the course of her therapy and convalescence. If we now cite just one more of Doris's productions, one she created about nine months prior to her severe disturbance, this single painting will make our observation even clearer. Illustration 16 is called "America" (reminiscent of Kafka's novel of the same name) and in its coloration and expressive power, comparable to those of Paul Klee, it is much superior to any of Doris's subsequent achievements.

Illustration 15

And yet, despite the total absence in it of everything living, and the sinister threats ("police"), closed doors, the inhospitable places ("bank," "police," "hotel," "coffee-bar"), that painting with its suppressed stars and the moon pushed aside, tragically projects the child's homelessness and, although it may not be the same, already presages her psychosis.

Ensuing developments after the dramatic shift

The obvious decline in the strength of graphic expression suggests the possibility that Doris's apparent recovery might instead be a "reorientation on a lower level" or even a yet unnoticeable "pseudo-recovery." One could arrive at such a surmise if one just looked at the pictures. But when one is necessarily occupied with the further development of the child and with everything the therapy includes in its broadest sense, one takes a different view of the shift in graphic representation: one regards it as a transfer of the place of action. Doris, at least for the moment but presumably for a longer period, is consigning what is happening to her no longer primarily to crayons and paper but instead to her interaction with her environment. And not even an aesthete could regret that. For what is now commencing is the most difficult part of the treatment, even if we take into account everything that the relational disturbance has already exacted from the child and her attendants. The reason is that we can no longer speak of "treatment" in the customary sense, any more than we can subsume what is now happening under some kind of conceivable illness.

The shift of the psychopathological symptoms
to the area of normal psychology
and the problems arising from the shift

Recollection of the psychosis

At first the condition subsequent to the "China" experience and the assimilation thereof looked promising. "Things are really going well for a few weeks," so the teacher notes: "She is again more industrious in school. And so gradually I can ask and demand a little more from her and need no longer fear that she will react peevishly to every little admonition . . . and then refuse to be talked to for some time. She is also eating better. . . ."

But soon thereafter mention is again made about "stubbornness and inflexibility." This kind of behavior affords the teacher no significant difficulties, above all no decisively troublesome problems concerning her attitude, since Miss Hüberli continues to speak of what seem to her to be "relapses": a connection between the girl's current conduct and the prior phase of "sickly conduct" seems apparent and its recognition does not obscure any specific problems. The girl's behavior is also such that her relationship to the earlier psychotic experience is still too urgent to be overlooked. So long as we are confronted with "relapses," our understanding with the teacher about the possibility and even necessity of such attacks is not difficult. Every aware person realizes that convalescence requires time and that it is not a condition but rather a course of development. Moreover, anyone acquainted with human development can be convinced of the extreme importance of the recollection of the psychosis, that is, a repetition of the psychotic conduct and how essential this is to its correlation with the personality and thereby the genuine integration of the psychotic experience.[5] It also follows that that kind of procedure is better because it is therapeutically more favorable than if the child left behind everything that had happened to her as though it had never been. The doctor in cooperation with the teacher may make all possible use of the understanding of everything that psychosis may signify or be correlated with. He is in a position to make clear that a patient, particularly a child, cannot discuss such matters until he has from time to time transferred himself back into that prior situation. He can also explain how very necessary a "fumbling around" that situation from various directions is. One can pave the way for understanding that for integration it is important not only that a child becomes aware of how she herself behaved at that time but, just as important, if not more so, that she should also learn what the rest of the world and especially the teacher would do, if the same thing recurred. In summary, one can count on the acceptance of everything that psychosis is or is alleged to be and can also count on understanding that, after the psychosis has subsided, a child, especially a deaf one, must repeat, re-experience, and "activate" the thrust she wants to have done with, even if it was a first and somewhat repressed one. And this is all the more true because the child cannot of course speak of it as could an adult with unimpaired hearing.[5]

Prevarication phase

The situation becomes difficult and on the whole different when the customary, though already unsuccessful, identification of the readiness to understand with an a priori type of forgiveness is forced unequivocally and with no discussion. But that is precisely what happens in the following situation.

"One of the older girls is missing two francs. I (note well the *I,* that is, the trusted teacher who has so often and lovingly stood by the girl) am missing my throat and vitamin tablets. I discover that Doris has the pills. She denies it, however, and it is shocking to see how straight she looks me in the face and how confident she is of her position." Thus, the child who hid herself, who was unable to show her face to anyone anymore, is now lying, indeed lying shamelessly, *into* her teacher's face *with* her own face.

The pills are discovered in Doris's possession. "Driven into a corner, she suddenly becomes aware that I know it, is frightened and commences to tremble and confesses. Later the matter of the money comes up. No, she maintains for a long time, I took only the tablets, I was thirsty during the night. I continue the questioning, she contradicts herself, I am able to score a point against her. Finally she is at her wits' end and confesses that on that Sunday . . . she had taken the money. She was unable to say why she had done it and was prepared to return the money. However, she pleads with me not to say anything about the matter to the other children, cries and throws herself into my arms. She is crestfallen and for the moment full of regrets." And in a bitterly critical way the teacher adds: "I am convinced, however, that she would never have admitted a thing if I had not been able to provide some evidence. . . . Later I observe how she counts the money rather obtrusively, in the presence of the others, and asks me whether her count checks. Obviously she does not want to keep the thing secret in spite of her request, indeed, she almost assumes an air of importance."

So now we are face to face with a completely new situation, as the teacher's reports indicate. Gone is the challenging insolence prevalent at the beginning of the psychosis and gone is the psychotic withdrawal. We are now directly, noticeably, and visibly facing a disposition toward cunning.

In clearly enunciating the name of this phenomenon we unequivocally introduce into the report the affective afflic-tion with which the term is basically bound up. It would be senseless to try to overlook this fact or even deny it. Even if this representation were to ignore it or even argue it away, the unquestionable and emphatic expression is in the teacher's report as a reflection of her attitude toward the child! "At times I lose a trick," concedes Miss Hüberli.

What is to be done in the face of such conduct? More important, it seems to me, is the negative formulation of the question, namely, that not what should be done but rather what one should refrain from doing should be determined in that kind of situation. We must simply refrain from doing anything that would destroy the tension of the situation. The tension results, as the basic tenor of Miss Hüberli's report clearly indicates, from the intensity of the emotion conditioning it. Nothing, therefore, could have been more wrong than wanting to eliminate that emotion or just to "redirect it." I have especially in mind the negative affect. Isolated for months, the child now challenges her teacher by stealing from her, precisely from *her*. And she literally lies *into her face*. Only in this cunning way is challenge possible for the child. But courage is lacking for the direct provocation. Doris does indeed *take up her position*, but not till she has "lied into her teacher's face." One might well feel how good the period of the psychosis with its unambiguous situation had been, a situation in which the question of one's stance toward the child was not the overriding problem!

There is no observable or suspected suffering present in the actual situation; nor is there any nosologically formulable "suffering" between Doris and her teacher. But now for the first time Doris is able, in connection with the confrontation of the question as to how one deals with this conduct, to experience directly and convincingly to herself how seriously she is being taken. Now also for the first time the question may become apparent to her as to whether a real confrontation is possible for her or whether she strikes other people as being so repulsive that they are not amenable to coming to terms with her. And Miss Hüberli once again stood the test in the face of this situation, no matter how difficult it may have been for her to have done so. The test was in that, despite the observable emotional affect, she manifested neither disappointment about the viciousness directed especially toward her, nor revulsion toward the child.

This is not to say that disappointment and revulsion were lacking. Both were mentioned in my discussion with Miss Hüberli. There would have had to be something amiss in our relationship, had she *not* mentioned both those feelings! But it would have been no less bad, had we avoided the analysis of what had occurred. What manifests itself here is healthy emotion. Compassion, disappointment, revulsion would on the contrary have been signs of sick emotion. In situations such as this, the point is not the question "Emotion, yes or no?" but rather what kind of an emotion is evoked. Sick or bad emotion means: "Now that is the kind of thanks I get for all that I have done for the child." Or, "Now the 'real character' of the child becomes manifest," followed by the frequently unexpressed comment, "All the preceding was merely a coverup," or "was only theatrics." Good and healthy emotion on the other hand says: "The girl is a stinker." This emotion says then what every angry good mother would have said spontaneously about her child in such a situation. It is spontaneous indignation against what has just occurred, though completely free of any regress to the peculiarity characterizing the earlier relation between the two or even to the mother's obligation to the child.

For Doris the precondition is given therewith also for the healthy coming to terms with her environment by way of a coming to terms with her teacher. The report of this progress reads: "During these weeks she is markedly less dependent and less in need of affection." And immediately following: "But as regards her education she still continues to give me great difficulty." That little "but" is basic. The remark that "she is markedly less dependent and less in need of affection" clearly indicates with the supplementary "but" of the following sentence that in and of themselves things might be easier for the teacher now that the child has reduced her consuming need of love, and the teacher admits freely and properly that the dependence was a burden to her, thereby proving that she did not need that burden as a confirmation of her competence.

The period of defiance

Scarcely were things getting easier for Doris when new difficulties arose. "Her typical behavior at this time: 1. She rejects something, indicates an unwillingness toward something else . . . . 2. Intensification: Is insistent, strong-headed, persistent, presses her demands, flies into a senseless rage . . . refuses to compromise, resists all punishment, all encouragement, all requests, all orders, persists in her defiant attitude. 3. Suddenly begins to realize . . . then cries hard, excuses herself and later wants to make amends. Seems then to be relieved of some compulsion. Promises she will now always behave and be reasonable."

This kind of conduct indicates that Doris is entering upon a new phase which we might call the "defiance stage." Her rage, earlier and falsely designated as "defiance" in the report, becomes *defiance* after she has mastered the stage of *cunning*. Wherein lies the difference between the three ways of conduct? Rage culminates in withdrawal. Cunning simulates dependence. Defiance on the other hand actually develops into dependence. Rage is sickly. Cunning is spiteful and as such relationally disturbing. Defiance is, contrariwise, healthy.

The defiant person puts on a bold front but also expects to find acceptance rather than rejection from the other fellow. Could such a thing happen in the case of a child like Doris, we subsequently ask ourselves, except by means of a detour through cunning?

The importance of the "defiance phase" for Doris is apparent from a notation according to which Doris asks her teacher: "Why do *I* actually hear nothing, but *you* do?" We cannot imagine this question put in any other way nor imagine an alternative approach except in a situation of defiance. This basic question which makes possible a coming to terms with one's own peculiarity contains a clear reproach to the effect that the intonation in putting the question makes impossible any over-hearing on the part of anyone who by virtue of his very ability to hear could *over*-hear. These questions, almost identical in their meaning, the one asking, "Why do I have this?" but now formulated in a slightly different way, that is, "Why do *I* hear nothing but *you* do?" reveal the difference between depressive resignation and defiant resistance. The former question is of course more convenient but the latter is prognostically more favorable, assuming, to be sure, that the person to whom the question is directed stands up to it.

The question—about it there can be no doubt in Doris's situation as in all other situations in which it arises—is intended as a challenge and consequently not as an occasion for reply. Every answer is accordingly false a priori if its intent is to satisfy the questioner (as well as the person questioned!). The answer is correct if it maintains the process of coming to terms. That is about all one can say to one's self, when one checks back on how one should deal with the question.

Two kinds of answers are not only false but also persistently harmful. The first kind says: "Thus did God want it." This type of answer is also false when formulated more neutrally: "God knew, of course, why he did it." Regardless of *who* provides that kind of answer, everyone answers falsely if he uses that statement. Theoretically, only a single exception would be imaginable, namely, this answer could be accepted under certain conditions by the questioner if it came from a deaf minister. But I cannot imagine a deaf person, let alone a deaf minister, who would have the courage to give such an answer to another person even if the minister had previously given it to himself. The other answer would be: "You lack hearing, but you do after all have healthy eyes that can see."

Both answers imply reproach which eliminates all coming to terms. They are phrased: "Just be satisfied. Don't rebel against the Creation. God has done well to give me, the listener, healthy ears." Or, "Other people have things much worse. Think of the blind." All this as though a man ever had anything by knowing that he did not have the right to come to terms with himself and his destiny because there are others who suffer a much crueler fate. The most dreadful thing that could happen after such an answer would probably be its acceptance by the questioner! Next to the manifestations of the feeling of superiority, expressed in the false answers alluded to, are the inferiority feelings of hearing persons, their feeling of helplessness and of bad conscience, moreover that *I,* the answering person, can hear all these "second most harmful" forms of conduct. Furthermore, these (customarily most frequent) answers utterly destroy the confrontation which, by virtue of such a question's having actually been put, was only then supposed to ensue.

So far as I am concerned, I know no better answer than the one Miss Hüberli and I gave. This answer is without doubt the stupidest one any intelligent person could invent. It is simply "I don't know." Its virtue is that though it can give the child neither satisfaction nor blame, it can provide occasion for continuing discussion.

The present state of affairs

In the meantime the child's development continues favorably. Doris is integrated into her community and is doing well in school. Her spirits generally are also good. The

period of defiance, however, is far from having been overcome and it is precisely at such times that we sense the great
insecurity in the child as well as in her teacher. The note
states: "She now excuses herself for every little thing, is
however absolutely unsatisfied till she realizes that I have
truly forgiven her for the misdemeanor. Then cries out: 'I'm
sorry, I'm sorry, do you hear?' till I embrace her. She throws
herself into my arms and holds me tight for some time."

This insecurity will probably never be wholly eliminated,
and perhaps it should not be. It seems to me to be in
conformity with the continuously recurring situation of being
rejected; Doris may possibly be unique in making rejection
by her environment tolerable simply by just not taking it for
granted but rather by seizing upon it.*

The improvement in the child's condition has received
welcome and promising corroboration from two interesting
observations from outsiders: someone among the school
personnel remarked quite casually that Doris did not smell,
indeed not at all. (I well remember that the earlier reference
was stink.) Inasmuch as the attendants at the school regularly provide intensive body care for the children, we may
not assume that this change in Doris is attributable to more
intensive bathing. Instead the generally accepted experience
that (unavowed) suffering gives off a smell probably finds
corroboration in this observation. The suffering probably did
not stop with the cessation of the olfactory secretion, but the
suffering is now acknowledged ("conscious") and thereby
amenable to analysis.

The remark that Doris smelled better is also important
for still another reason. A person who stinks is unsympathetic and more so if his odor is not experienced at all as such

* I note some evidence that this process is now going on in Doris because a
noticeable disquietude, viewed with alarm by some, has recently occurred in the
child in consequence of sex education. Is it necessary to mention that such a
reaction is more reassuring because it is "more natural" and also prognostically
more favorable than complete indifference would be?

by himself or by the "receiver" (not the perceiver, however). The stinking suffering is thus imparted, in the most original sense of the term, unconsciously. Hence, if Doris now smells better, then her relational disturbance has begun to dissipate at the point where it, in a most perfidious way because unrecognized and therefore impervious to influence from both sides, had earlier become effective.

Above and beyond this, occasional visitors to the school expressed their astonishment (to the secretary, not the doctor) about how nice Doris had "suddenly" become.

Unfortunately this development will not continue. It does, however, constitute an encouragement in the mastery of subsequent difficulties and disappointments which we shall confront in appropriate fashion but which we shall never be able to prevent.*

* Two years have passed between the completion of the manuscript and the typesetting (1968). In the interim Doris was confirmed. She has remained a healthy, integrated girl and will shortly make her choice of occupation.

III. Inferences and Conclusions

By selecting certain significant situations illustrating the peculiarity of the problem and thereby omitting pragmatic descriptions of the developmental and therapeutic phases, we have presented the report of the illness and treatment of a child suffering from manifold relational difficulties. What can we learn from the report in general and in particular?

Generalities

The psychotherapeutic situation appears spontaneously in an ordered group which makes candid speech possible. The therapist can and indeed should remain in the background. His presence rather than his activity is important.

The attitude of the therapist could hardly be better demonstrated anywhere than in those situations which Doris reveals to him either in her graphic representations or in her dreams. Wherever he appears as St. Nicholas, as Eskimo, as clown, or as mandarin (designated in part as such by the child in those very words), he invariably assumes a clearly peripheral position, that is, he never occupies the center of the stage. He continues, however, to remain where he belongs in the community which he does not try to suppress but rather tries to hold together and to supplement.

Hence, the "situation of transference" is splintered in a different way, certainly, from the one we customarily encounter in group therapy. The therapist is indeed not the grey eminence in the background. Instead he functions indirectly, not kept secret from the child, but in general inconspicuously, through the supervisors, whose place the child knows and has known since entering the school, and whose rank in her microcosm she understands.

Let me add, however, that of the personnel involved in treating Doris, I alone am directly and professionally knowledgeable in psychoanalysis. The other personnel have had no direct professional training in that field. Had that not been the case, then certainly many other things would have happened in the therapy, whether for good or bad I cannot say with any certainty. One can, however, maintain with some assurance that psychological "interests" and "knowledge" without ongoing meetings among the personnel involved in the treatment would not only have been worthless but actually harmful.

Specifics

Whatever we experienced with and about Doris is not in context. But in the course of certain cardinal situations it has been alluded to and acted upon in context. We shall not mention the matter again. Along with the development and therapy we also mentioned the ideas and suggestions that arose in relation to individual situations. This kind of description would, we hope, anticipate the illusory conception that so often leads to disillusionment and according to which incontrovertible truth is accorded to "pure casuistry" and to the description of that which obviously "was."

It seemed to me more truthful to describe what we were thinking from time to time and what particulars we observed or failed to see than to assert what I believed I had seen as being what "really was," as though anyone really and seriously could see such things and, above all, be in a position to talk freely about them.

We should, however, be clear about three questions, which we therefore must tackle separately and answer as far as is possible. The three questions are:

What was Doris suffering from?

Wherein lay the uniqueness of Doris's treatment?

How and to what extent and with what right can we now pronounce the present condition of the child as cured?

The affliction

The question of what Doris was suffering from cannot be answered directly. For Doris was not suffering from something, that is, from something that came at her without her being able to describe it to herself or our being able to describe it to ourselves.

Nor was Doris a victim of something, in any case not from birth on and certainly not since the beginning of her psychotic disturbance. To persuade her that she suffered from or with "something," indeed was really capable of suffering with something, was already a piece of psychotherapy and, indeed, the most decisive and daring and divisive part of the entire psychotherapy.

This fact is of principal importance to the therapeutic attitude in the situation described here. The child was able to attain distance toward *something*, could talk about *something*, and thereby distinguish herself from *something*. This *something* always meant something that could be casually referred to as "suffering" only until she was able to convert or transmute that *which she herself was* into something she *had* or *has* and would from now on and always, irrevocably and unchangeably, have and keep. The basic change lies in the fact that she now *has it* and no longer *is it.*

It was difficult to achieve reaching the stage of "suffering beneath suffering," because precisely those locations at which and by means of which a human being experiences and confirms himself in his being and his being so are sick: for example, *hearing* in the sense of hearing one's self, a phenomenon corroborated by the reply coming from without, and *seeing,* not in the customary sense of optical perception (which still remains intact) but rather in the sense of self-confirmation which a human being continuously experiences from the attitude of his environment toward his appearance [*Aus-sehen*].

The nature of Doris's illness is conditioned by the combination of her disfigurement with her deafness and not by the nosological entity of the congenitally conditioned affliction. Thus, we are not dealing with specific forms of suffering or expression for a Klein-Waardenburg syndrome.

This combination of two relational disturbances, namely, deafness and disfigurement (and we have demonstrated why a special position belongs to *facial* disfigurement), causes special tragedy. It is neither possible nor feasible to provide a scale for measuring the "extent or degree of tragedy," but still we must point to the different and relationally more disturbing way in which the combination of *deafness-disfigurement* functions when compared to the combination of *deafness-blindness.*

For blindness does not merely intensify the relational disturbance, which is conditioned in deafness, but even mitigates, indeed *compensates,* in certain areas the one with the other. Blindness, associated with deafness, selects the disturbing, confusing, defensive answers that continuously re-echo to the deaf person. But disfigurement does not mitigate, nor does it select anything out. Indeed and to the contrary, whatever bewilderment deafness may produce in the person opposite him, disfigurement increases it.

The compassion for which the deaf-blind person may hope at a first encounter, a situation which can by means of the combined relational disturbances easily occur in an unpremeditated way and thereby leave time for adaptation, is made impossible by the stormy, unprepared encounter between the healthy person and the deaf-disfigured one. The first reaction of the healthy person when he directly and without preparation encounters the deaf-disfigured child is consequently not compassion but instantaneous bewilderment, sometimes astonishment, and in consequence revulsion.

This is the situation we understand as elementary relational disturbance. One of its primary characteristics is the extraordinary fact that we cannot say whose relationship is disturbed, that of the obviously handicapped person or that of the healthy one facing him.

In response to stimuli of this kind Doris appeared in various forms of behavior, as previously described.

The course of development

The following sequence of phenomena, that is, Doris's modes of conduct, also characterizes the course and history of her illness, that is, her suffering and treatment:

1. At first the little girl was comical in her relational disturbance. Like little Punch she lived out her disturbance playfully.

2. When that was no longer possible, she became impudent, shameless, obtrusive. Through her conduct she anticipated what her appearance would directly have produced anyway.

3. The continuing severe traumatizations that developed for Doris produced an angry attitude far in excess of what we encounter as "pouting" in the development of healthy children.

4. Since there were no alternatives to such an attitude, the final result was complete withdrawal. At this point psychotherapy began.

5. After that, the withdrawal, subsequent to an interim of attentiveness, was replaced by cunningness.

6. Finally, then, obstinacy set in.

We are still in this phase and it will still require some time before decisions and discussions inherent in and made feasible by it develop to a point at which a free relationship becomes possible.

The phase of withdrawal seems to me now to be identical with the initial stage of psychosis for which many terms can be found. However one might designate that situation, I am convinced that the affliction would in weeks or months have culminated in a chronic catatonic condition.

Of course, one can maintain that the favorable development which the therapeutic team sought to follow and apply from the withdrawal phase on was already present in a nutshell, so to speak. But with whose help was the nut supposed to be cracked? We can learn nothing from the attitude of the psychotherapist regarding either which factors necessarily and naturally belong together spatially in the sense of the syndrome or what relates to what conditionally in temporal sequence.

The six developmental phases afford us no help in formulating an opinion about *what* the child had suffered *from*. However, they do point out *how* she suffered and how she manifested her suffering and brought it to the attention of others.

Meanwhile there is no demonstrable relationship between the divulging of her suffering by the child, on the one hand,

and the excessiveness of the suffering, on the other. Possibly, indeed very probably, the suffering would have been less had Doris succumbed to her psychosis.

The uniqueness of the treatment

The uniqueness of the treatment is conditioned by the uniqueness of the child. The child's uniqueness may briefly be described thus: Doris with her illness, her nature together with her relational disturbance, and her being—all are identical with her expression. "Insight" or "knowledge" could not be gained in any of the usual ways, nor could "distancing" from herself or from anything else.

Apart from this, Doris had avoided the usual procedures of child psychotherapy, play therapy, for example. And the reason the customary procedures used in the active therapy of psychosis were not applied has already been explained in our discussion of the *réalisation symbolique*.

The complete identity of being and expression had to be the determining factor for the therapy. In her most difficult periods, however, Doris has shunned expression therapy in the contemporary sense of that term as self-projection into something or, in less prejudicial terms, as self-expression by some means, such as graphics. Above all, however, it was impossible to approach such a severe relational disturbance indirectly through the expression therapy. Moreover, there was nothing having to do with expression in the disturbance itself. There was absolutely nothing there that could have expressed itself *in* something or *by means of* something. Everything came directly at one without any kind of articulation or symbolism. How then could any kind of therapeutic procedure—speech, writing, or symbolic treatment—utilizing expression, count on winning acceptance from Doris?

Everything with which Doris approached us was (and this we cannot overemphasize) anything but expression; it was, instead, the very being of the child. It is no less possible to understand or approach facial disfigurement as "facial expression" than to understand what the child "had to say" as expression.

One might, indeed, have been able to practice "expression therapy" with Doris in the customary sense of that term. One could have undertaken drawing, modeling, or anything else. Or one could have talked with the child and discussed almost anything with her, even her trouble. But this kind of therapy would have bypassed the direct, spontaneously occurring demand [*AN-spruch*] of her suffering.

One had to confront the demand of the girl just as directly as she herself confronted the outsider with it. Her demand resists all efforts to read or hear something *into* or *out of* it. It insists solely on making a demand to the demand.

To confront the demand in a demanding way is consequently so difficult because the healthy outsider is taken unawares by it. The hearing person is immediately rendered speechless when he encounters an excited deaf person. Strange as it may sound, the situation is precisely the reverse of what one might ordinarily expect, that is, speechlessness lies with the hearing-speaking person and not with the deaf person. It is for this reason, of course, that there is an inclination, so relationally destructive, on the part of the hearing person to avoid a psychological explanation of the person he encounters when he confronts that kind of threatening, and frightening, and isolating phenomenon. This is especially true when he is doubly confronted by threatening danger, that is, in the aural and in the visual realm.

Proceeding from our awareness of the significance of the situation of a child thus afflicted relationally and of what she wants from us, we first of all put aside everything that might have "mediated" between the two of us, Doris and me. The relationship with the girl was established as immediate and as direct as could be imagined for both partners, namely, by means of face-to-face confrontation and then by an echoing and repeating of Doris's statements.

The intention to understand was second in importance to the wish to relate to one another. At first I did not try to understand whatever Doris had *to say* or express or discuss. Only what she said and the manner of her doing so were of significance from the very first and for a long time thereafter. We made no effort to ascertain from time to time what Doris meant, nor did we attempt to obtain from her utterances some clarification of her life history and pre-psychotic living conditions regardless of what "significance" these things might have concerning her conduct or what she said. Our sole and only immediate concern was to create and to preserve relatedness in its most intensive form and at any price.

By *relatedness* we mean here the totality of all those emanations of a human being that help him to find himself, to corroborate his awareness of his being and of his self, that is, to prevent him from losing himself. By means of this concept and the procedure derived from it, we countered the oft recurring tendency toward isolation, to wit, the self-surrender of Doris.

Now, relatedness can be controlled and kept moving in many quite different ways, especially by varying intensity. Of all the possible ways of relating we chose the most vital one, namely, confrontation (*frons*–Latin for forehead) in its most original and most peculiar way. Confrontation means standing face-to-face in complete similarity of kind and equivalence and with the exclusion of all intermediate ties. This kind of confrontation is to be understood as follows:

1. *Direct confrontation,* which means the permanent ex-

clusion of everything that could effect the mutual distraction of the two partners to another and third thing. Only we two, in the present case Doris and I, remain in the state of relatedness.

2. *Homologous relation,* whereby the locales by means of which and toward which we have related ourselves are in the case of Doris and me exactly identical, for the relating occurred from face to face and not from the mouth to the ear, viz., heterologously, or from two otherwise unlike locales.*

This kind of direct-homologous relation is of such intensity that it tends continuously to diminish or at least shift into a less tense kind of mutual relatedness. Accordingly, it can maintain itself only for a limited time, indeed, only for the period of a mutual glance or for the flick of an eyelash. Because of the limited time available for this kind of relatedness it must be experienced with all the intensity it is capable of.

We sought to practice this kind of relatedness by communicating through "echoes," thus preserving the relationship by speaking the patient's jargon. This kind of encounter made expression possible; the expression then, because it was reciprocally structured, led to discussion.

By reference to this kind of procedure we have touched upon a basic problem of psychotherapy, namely, the question whether, how, and to what extent expression solely by means of echoing and repeating or by means of creating and recreating is at all possible. Do we not find convincing evidence that psychotherapy in every form of depression is very difficult, some even say impossible, given a case according to which the creating-recreating of the depression is frustrating for the patient as well as for the psychotherapist because it can be misunderstood as a travesty? Indeed, how

* These terms and concepts are explained in a more detailed way in my *Versuch über die Elemente der Beziehung.*[12]

should one create-recreate a depression without letting it reach its reciprocal potential through the agency of patients and therapists or letting it become a travesty?

Be that as it may, only the creating-recreating is able in all forms of relational disturbance to restore the disturbed relationship. At times the possibility of inducing such voiding or expression must be forced. Doris also had attempted to shun it in trying to turn away from me.

I once needed to confront another patient, severely disfigured as the result of brain surgery, by taking away her mirror, which she used over and over again to examine her disfigurement. I said to her: "Let's forget about the mirror and just look at *each other*." Her relational disturbance was eliminated by this means and her relatedness restored, although it followed an initial stormy confrontation.

This kind of relationship is surely much less "warm" than the various kinds of careful and protective therapy, but it is equally certain that it is more vital. All the usual procedures of protective and permissive therapy are in essence heterologous, that is, they never proceed in exactly the same way. All of them recognize one person who protects and fosters and the second person who is protected and fostered. How very much one felt the compulsion to give this unhappy child what she never had had in life! But it would surely have been improper to have acceded to this spontaneous inclination. As extremely tragic as it is, and incidentally that is precisely the essence of tragedy, Doris would probably have persisted even more in her isolation in the face of a protective therapy for which she was unprepared simply because she had never been "prepared" for it. Experience demonstrates, and especially the experience with children severely afflicted with this kind of relational disturbance, that human beings must without exception be prepared for everything including being protected.

It was a favorable circumstance that Doris found security

with her teacher as soon as she had become receptive to the idea. This being the case, an additional advantage accrued because the protective posture was experienced in a discreet and never in an impetuous way.

This intensive and tense kind of relationship made impossible the child's flights from her environment which she previously had sought and found. Meanwhile it must be apparent that this kind of mutual relatedness could be created and maintained only for a short time, namely, as already stated, for as long as' the wink of an eyelash. Accordingly, it would never have been possible nor even probable to let the treatment come to an end in this way. Each time the child would have fallen "into a vacuum," particularly since her therapy required her to return to her group. We simply could not permit her to walk away from this relationship and its almost trancelike effectiveness.

Therefore, after such intensive and direct confrontation we had to find some kind of "transition" to what one might call the conventional. In accordance with what we have been saying, this could happen only by severing the reciprocal experiencing by means of the mutual experiencing of something. This occurred by our drawing on the blackboard, later by eating together, and subsequently, horrible to say, by doing Doris's school lessons together. In this way we prepared the return to normal living and to the companionship of the other children.

It might seem peculiar that in our discussions so far we have not once hinted at any special "technique" or "methodology" for coming to an understanding with deaf children. Indeed, little need be said about that. A good understanding of how deaf people speak and understand and how one talks with them is naturally indispensable for conversing with them. Anything beyond this kind of competence would probably be not only superfluous but actually obstructive for the psychotherapist. Too precise cultivation of language, overly tender treatment of the linguistic expression of the deaf, even persistence regarding what has been said, all such disturb the therapeutic relationship (incidentally, not only for the deaf!). The cultivation of language is the business of the teacher of the deaf with whose competence the psychotherapist never concerns himself.

A certain general experience in intercourse with the handicapped is also helpful for the psychotherapy of a child so severely afflicted with a relational disturbance, for then the spontaneous embarrassment of the healthy person, which the child would sense immediately (and exploit!), would not happen to the therapist. But more dangerous than this kind of embarrassment would be the frequently observable tendency of the therapist at first to take in a biased way the part of his afflicted protégé and, subsequently, because of the inevitable disappointments, assume the very opposite kind of attitude toward and with the child. "Participation without partisanship" is therefore the slogan of the program for which we have here attempted to provide some guidelines.

In spite of all the foregoing information we do not wish the thought to arise that all this was done merely to describe an unusually difficult treatment. We are well aware that much of the suffering and related therapy (whose peculiarity recurs frequently in other cases of elementary relational disturbance) is not more difficult but instead simpler than conventional therapies. The intensity especially but, even more, the directness with which the suffering confronted us (or sought to escape us), the persistent "here and right now" not only excused us from penetrating but forbade us from "penetrating the depths," indeed penetrating two-dimensional depths such as the "soul strata" and the early life history. Concerning the *"area* of the psyche," it should not and could not be penetrated because Doris brings us her total suffering legibly written on her forehead and by stammering or speaking with her mouth (not in the what but in the how). Because of this, the nature of the emotional affect enabled us to dispense with a discussion of her life history. After all, we did experience the psychosis together with Doris essentially from its inception and that certainly facilitated its treatment. And as for the experiences of her early childhood, they were, because of the very nature of her suffering, continuously and unquestionably present in its actual form.

Discussion of Doris's conduct upon conclusion of the therapy

Our concluding remark about how much is and remains present leads us finally to our last question, namely, whether and to what extent we may in general speak of a cure.

The following observation, apparently or actually trivial, must serve as a preface: Doris is deaf and disfigured and she will remain that way. Nothing can ever change that.

This fact demands a specific attitude toward and a special conception of what constitute ultimate convalescence or healing in a terminal situation thus conditioned by deafness and disfigurement.

The two aspects of cure

These are situations in which the attitude toward cure differs between the therapist and the patient. This situation requires earnest reflection lest it should actually happen that the therapist pronounces his patient cured whereas the patient is quite convinced that he is not. The reverse might also be possible, and it happens not infrequently, that the patient insists he is cured whereas the doctor regards him as not cured. Accordingly, any pronouncement about a cure must take into account two different points of view: a) that of the patient, and b) that of the therapist.

The question as to which of the two points of view is "correct" must naturally remain moot. Basically it is impossible even to raise the question, for there is no available basis for determining the competence requisite for answering it. But what is involved is not simply the proper answer but rather that the point of departure and the point of execution of the two opposing partners become clear.

The course of Doris's psychosis and her development under therapy now clearly demonstrate to us what is involved for the patient so as to enable and allow him to experience himself as cured.

Awareness of health

How is Doris today? She performs the tasks assigned her and she utilizes the possibilities available to her within her limitations. She is a regular student and a beloved companion within the circle of the other deaf children. She has friends but also potential opponents. She is reserved, almost shy, toward people who can hear and generally toward all strangers. But she lets herself be talked to and then reveals herself as surprisingly free. In the presence of those she knows, Miss Hüberli, for example, or myself, she can become pert and even impudent, especially toward her teacher. And at times there are periods that anxiously and emphatically again recall the earlier experiences. It was just such a phase we briefly alluded to earlier as taking place in connection with sex education.

We should now like to suggest a designation for what has been described. What is developing now in Doris is the struggle for awareness of health, that is, a kind of health that knows how healthy it is. A person who has awareness of health knows how he is, who he is, but also knows how and who he can never be.[11]

That does not mean, however, that he "knows his place." Quite the contrary, for he fights and he spits. This kind of health also has nothing to do with the "ability to suffer." A person with awareness of health accordingly offers little support for every edifying activity. Awareness of health does not mean: Look here, I am deaf and disfigured, but still I am happy. The man with awareness of health has also not "accepted himself." How could he really accept himself inasmuch as that which is to be accepted coincides with that which accepts?

Awareness of health is not a condition but a process of development or, more precisely stated, a development whose course can be maintained only so long as it knows the place where it can take place. Therein surely lies a highly suspect observation, but we do better to admit it than to ignore it. Nobody can guarantee a child such as Doris health per se or even general and continuing health. Doris needs people by whom she is not only accepted but who also take her seriously, and that means people who not only generally provide affection for her but who she also knows with certainty will not withdraw that affection when she is demanding or exasperating.

An essential and decisive characteristic of awareness of health is its conviction, comparatively speaking, that "I am thus and so" and not only "I am different" from the others. And that is pertinent because the person who constantly reminds himself of his differentness always wants to be like the others, that is, the majority of healthy people. The person with awareness of health is well disposed to himself. But being well disposed to himself can never remain just a condition. It must constantly prove itself over and over again.

Thus, the man aware of his health is not a comfortable partner. But for whose benefit ought he to be so? He is, in fact, unsuitable as a projection point for all of the humanitarian activities of his environment.

The China dream represented an important stage on the way to awareness of health. But it was after all only a stage, just as anything which is formulated and presented in pictures always marks the conclusion of one stage and the beginning of a new stage. When awareness of health becomes certainty, it raises some new questions. This observation leads to an extraordinary conclusion, namely, that the person with awareness of health knows a lot but he never knows that he is healthy. For him whatever is commonly regarded as health, such as the state of self-confidence, of the conviction that one can be only like this one person is, has lost its validity. Health to him is something only comparative and obviously still questionable.

Plain ordinary experience, of course, teaches us to be very cautious, particularly in the psychotherapy of psychoses, be they of schizophrenic or affective psychotic character, whenever a former psychotic with complete self-assurance declares himself completely healthy. All too often in such cases the possibility of a relapse is not too far removed. Awareness of health always excludes itself from certainty. It may be unique but this experience is valid for the situation of the convalescence of a thirteen-year-old girl. That convalescence occurs in a child simultaneously with the loss of naïveté, indeed *must* so occur, a condition we may well regret but cannot change.

The adequate cure

What kinds of possibilities are available to the psychotherapist (from his point of view) for evaluating Doris's present situation? We must first of all answer this question with a negative formulation: it is not permissible to derive the criteria for judging the cure from the thought system of psychotherapy (regardless of the usage). This principle is valid for strictly logical reasons and not because of psychotherapeutic laws. The value and position of a matter cannot be judged or evaluated within the framework of a system of which it is a part. This is true in general. We are in no position to make statements about music with notes, or statements about the nature of mathematics with figures, or statements about painting with colors. The same is true of psychotherapeutics. To evaluate Doris's success we cannot, for example, inquire as to how matters stand regarding transference or counter-transference, nor do we gain a clear insight into the healing of the child by determining which phase of development has now been reached in her. If we want to learn the current state of the girl's convalescence, we need to proceed according to the principles of a nonpsychotherapeutic system.

That kind of system results spontaneously when we proceed to measure her *actual* condition now as compared with her condition at the beginning of the therapy. That kind of procedure will never result in a judgment of "absolute cure" or "cure per se." Instead, this procedure has only a relative cure, that is, a cure related to and measured by what has preceded. Thus, the question of the extent and soundness of the cure must be directed toward the question of whether and to what extent the prior situation has become integrated or, to speak in more neutral terms, what has happened to the prior condition.

In this view there is no such thing as absolute cure, and no *restitutio ad integrum* in conventional medical terms. Where and when and how could we expect an *integrum* in a child such as Doris? Her cure can only be understood as an *adequate cure.* Adequate in that context means in comparison with her prior condition, and that in turn means that the prior disturbance has been restructured.

One might, theoretically at least, assume that Doris now

conducts herself as all other children do, that is, as all other *deaf* children do. But this is not the case. Doris is different from the other children of her age in this school for the deaf. She is more demanding, more jealous, much more serious, and at times more impudent than the other children in her group. Thus, we still find present what Doris revealed in her psychosis, although in a socially more acceptable way and, for Doris herself, in a way that can be better coordinated with living.

This kind of conduct seems to me to reflect the adequate cure of the peculiar psychosis which Doris suffered. Everything is somehow still discernible. Everything must continue to be relived. There can be no talk of a *restitutio ad integrum,* all the more so because an *integrum* never existed.

But why should not this adequate cure be regarded as acceptable and as the better form of cure, better, that is, than the attainment of a condition striking to the least conceivable degree? Because this kind of living and conduct provides the greatest possible guarantee that the earlier disturbance will not recur. This kind of cure as we now see in Doris is the natural one, for every disturbance that manifests the "biologically highest possible" extreme of stringency, that is, is neither too weak to be worked upon nor too strong to destroy, leaves behind perennial confrontation and discussion as adequate cure in precisely the way we have observed in consequence of this psychosis.[6]

The fact that Doris feels well *now* does not of itself afford anything by way of prognosis. But yet something accrues from it which we might formulate as the *binding law of the single instance.* The child has been furtively ill but subsequently got well. Whatever was possible once basically implies possibilities for the future, and an obligation for the therapist! Just as we can say of someone who once had, let us say, an artistic inspiration that that creative talent lies imminent in him somewhere and will always remain there, so we can also maintain that, on the basis of the *one* convalescence, Doris is competent and is enough cured to lead a life tolerable for her and her environment regardless of what changes in her conduct may occur in the future.

The question as to whether the circumstances, which guarantee that kind of life and which we have described here, can be preserved must remain moot.

Bibliography

1. Adler, A. *Studie über Minderwertigkeit von Organen.* Munich: Bergmann, 1927.
2. Basilier, T. "Reflexionen über Gehörverlust und Persönlichkeitsentwicklung." *Neue Bl. Taubstummenbildung* 19 (1965): 101.
3a. Bleuler, E. *Unbewusste Gemeinheiten.* Munich: Reinhardt, 1906.
3b. ——————. *Dementia praecox oder Gruppe der Schizophrenien.* Leipzig/Vienna: Deuticke, 1911.
4. Bodenheimer, A. R. "Über das psychische Agens." *Psyche* 9 (1955): 390–98.
5. ——————. *Erlebnisgestaltung. Darstellung eines Verfahrens zur Psychotherapie von Psychosen.* Basel: Schwabe, 1957.
6. ——————. "Das Bild der geheilten Depression." *J. Psychol. Psychother. med. Anthropol.* 12 (1965): 305–19.
7. ——————. "Was lehrt uns der Verfolgungswahn der Schwerhörigen als Paradigma der Psychosen?" *Schweiz. Arch. Neurol. Neurochir. Psychiat.* 91/I (1962): 129–37.
8. ——————. "Das Wesen des Schwerhörigen-Verfolgungswahnes und das Verständnis der Psychosen." *Schweiz. Arch. Neurol. Neurochir. Psychiat.* 93/II (1964): 413–15.
9. ——————. "Was bedeutet Sehen?—Was heisst blind Sein?" *J. Psychol. Psychother. med. Anthropol.* 13 (1966): 213–25.
10. ——————. *Der Schwerhörige und seine Umwelt. Mbl. BSSV* 10 (1966); appeared as separate publication.
11. ——————. "Die Begegnung der Umwelt mit der Krankheit." In *Der Mensch in der Begegnung,* edited by A. Friedemann. Bern: Huber, 1967, pp. 52–90.
12. ——————. *Versuch über die Elemente der Beziehung.* Basel: Schwabe, 1967.

13. —————————. "Die psychotherapeutische Beziehung mit dem gehörlosen Kinde." *Prax. Kinderpsychol.* 17 (1968): 87–97.
14. v. Feuchtersleben, E. *Zur Diätetik der Seele.* Berlin o. J.: Deutsche Bibliothek (1st ed., 1849).
15. Fromm-Reichmann, F. "Problems of therapeutic management in a psychoanalytic hospital." *Psychoanal. Quart.* 16 (1947): 325.
16. —————————. "Notes on the development of treatment of schizophrenics by psychoanalytic psychotherapy." *Psychiatry* 11 (1948): 263.
17. Klein, D. Albinisme partiel (leucisme) ave surdi-mutité, blépharophimose." *Helvet. paediat. Acta* 5 (1950): 38–57.
18. Koch, K. *Der Baum-Test. Der Baumzeichen-Versuch als psychodiagnostisches Hilfsmittel.* Bern: Huber, 1949.
19. Plessner, H. *Die Einheit der Sinne. Grundlinien einer Aesthesiologie der Sinne.* Reprint of 1st ed. Bonn: Bouvier, 1965.
20. Ringli, G. "Die Entwicklung des Schülerbestandes der Taubstummenanstalt Zürich." *Neue Bl. Taubstummenbildung* 19 (1965): 260.
21. —————————. "Die Mitarbeit des Psychotherapeuten in der Taubstummenschule." *Prax. Kinderpsychol.* 17 (1968): 97–98.
22. Séchehaye, M. A. *Die symbolische Wunscherfüllung. Darstellung einer neuen psychotherapeutischen Methode und Tagebuch der Kranken.* Bern: Huber, 1955.
23. —————————. *Introduction à une psychothérapie des schizophrènes.* Paris: Presses Universitaires de France, 1954.
24. Waardenburg, P. J. "A new syndrome combining developmental anomalies of the eyelids, eyebrows, and nose root with pigmentary defects of the iris and head hair and with congenital deafness." *Amer. J. hum. Genet.* 3 (1951): 195–253.
25. Zulliger, H. *Schwierige Kinder.* 4th ed. Bern: Huber, 1958.

Postscript to the American Edition

Several years have passed since the publication of the German edition of this little book. Hence, several additional and complementary observations are in order.

First, I should like to update my report about the girl whose situation is the subject of my book. Doris is, of course, no longer a child. She has grown up and has indeed become an attractive teenager with a special kind of charm. Furthermore, she discharges all of her day-to-day obligations in a competent manner. Her disfigurement, however, continues to reflect a remarkable situation. For example, once after a meeting with some other young people she confessed, "They were frightened of me." She is able to make this kind of assertion so dispassionately that it scares one. And yet that she can do so corroborates the adequacy of her cure and her awareness of health. After all, how else might she be expected to react adequately to her kind of situation?

The therapy and cure have been consummated. This fact is not cited here to corroborate the significance of some specific theory or idea or therapy. It is intended solely as a supplementary report that I feel I probably owe my readers.

I wish that I could report of having received some constructive critical responses to the German edition. Such reactions might have contributed to a better understanding of some matters I may have presented obscurely or even incorrectly. Alas, I received no such useful critical reactions, much to my own and my readers' surprise and disappointment. This is indeed regrettable, gratifying as many comments of approval have been.

Those criticisms I did receive, however, came from people who, I regret to say, were simply ill-informed and incapable of any understanding. I was accused, for example, of a grave omission because I took no photographs of the child. Allegedly I should have provided all kinds of photographs: front views, side views, back views, and both nude and fully dressed ones. These critics also asserted that I should have submitted a precise neurostatus in addition to the results of certain psychological tests, such as abdominal reflexes, patellar reflexes, electroencephalograms, pneumoencephalograms, even a Rorschach and a Thematic Apperception test. There are, of course, still other possibilities for torturing the child. But I am still mindful of what occurred at the X-ray examination, which warned us that it would not contribute to any helpful understanding, but, on the contrary, could do much harm. Despite that unfortunate experience, the alleged critical omissions probably conform to what some people regard as science or to what they expect from science.

Anything else could hardly be expected. Much more impressive is the fact that so unspectacular a case, viewed both in terms of its origin and subsequent development, should nonetheless have generated a certain amount of interest. That it did so surprised me and I can offer only three possible explanations:

1. Doris's history might perhaps illustrate that understanding is possible even when comprehension is completely absent.
2. Because of its simple structuring and the obviousness of the therapeutic problem, Doris's case can perhaps contribute suggestions and understanding for psy-

chotherapeutic problems of a radically different kind and for their respective solutions.

3. Above and beyond all else, however, it might well be that Doris has provided the answer to questions we could otherwise not come by. All of us, children of this strange period of history, have been regarded as deformed and noisy tin drummers (alluding, of course, to Gunter Grass's novel *The Tin Drum* [1959]).

Nothing, factual or aesthetic, can contradict this interpretation of our age or manage to change the human image consonant with it unless it be that the experience of our disfigured and deaf little girl constitutes some kind of breakthrough—not, to be sure, to some new image of mankind. Indeed, we do not all require an image different from the one presently so appropriate to us. What we do need, however, is a preparedness for finding our way about in that very image.

I wish to take this opportunity to thank the teaching staff of Wayne State University, above all, my friend Dr. John Tenny and his coworkers, for their kind invitation to lecture at the Department for Special Education during the summer term 1967, and for the unforgettable hospitality which I received on that occasion.

Tel-Hashomer, Israel   A. R. B.
Autumn 1973

Aron Ronald Bodenheimer, formerly consultant, University Hospital, Zurich, and head of the service for the deaf, Zurich, is currently director of the department of psychiatry and psychotherapy, H. Sheba Medical Centre, University of Tel Aviv Medical School, Israel. He received the M.D. degree (1949) and specialist in psychiatry and psychotherapy (1954) from the University of Basel. He has published extensively in the field, mostly in German.

Harold A. Basilius is professor emeritus of German, Wayne State University, and former director of the Wayne State University Press.

The manuscript was edited by Marguerite C. Wallace. The book was designed by Richard Kinney. The typeface for the text is CRT Times Roman, the design of which was supervised by Stanley Morison; and the display faces are Optima, designed by Herman Zapf in 1958, and Stack.

The text is printed on Nashoba text paper and the book is bound in Linson Products' Linson 2 cloth over binders boards. Manufactured in the United States of America.